·❖·HOG WILD!·❖·

HOG WILD!

A Delectable Collection of Over 100
Delicious Pork Recipes . . . & Delightful Pig Lore

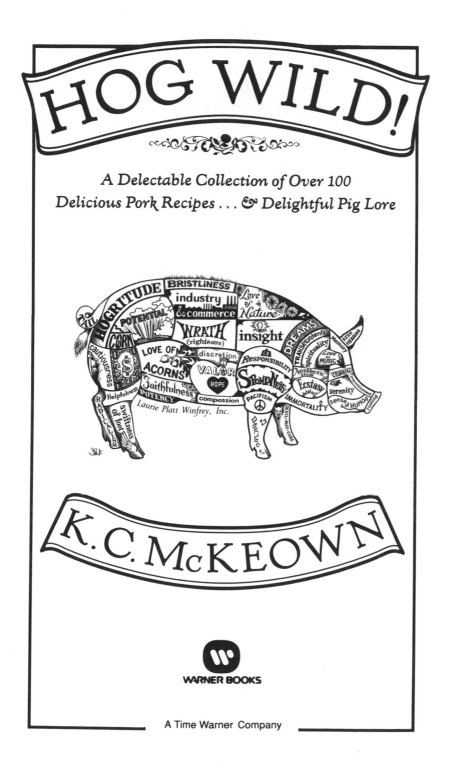

Laurie Platt Winfrey, Inc.

K.C. McKEOWN

WARNER BOOKS

A Time Warner Company

Warner Books, Inc., 1271 Avenue of the Americas, New York, N.Y. 10020

W A Time Warner Company

Printed in the United States of America
First printing: September 1992
10 9 8 7 6 5 4 3 2 1

Library of Congress Cataloging-in-Publication Data

McKeown, K. C.
    Hog wild! / K.C. McKeown.
      p.   cm.
    Includes bibliographical references (p.   ) and index.
    ISBN 0-446-39250-2
    1. Cookery (Pork) I. Title.
TX749.5.P67M35   1992   92-3892
641.6′64—dc20   CIP

Book design by Giorgetta Bell McRee
Cover design by Mario Pulice
Cover illustration by John Craig

For Caitlin

CONTENTS

"On each side of the whole length of Broadway were booths and stands . . . and on which were displayed small plates of oysters, clams sweltering in the hot sun, pineapples, boiled hams, pies, puddings, barley sugar and other indescribables. But what was remarkable, Broadway being three miles long, and the booths lining each side of it, in every booth there was a roast pig, large or small, as the center attraction. Six miles of roast pig! and that in New York City alone; and roast pig in every other city, town, hamlet and village in the Union. What association can there be between roast pig and independence?"

—CAPTAIN FREDERICK MARRYAT,
visiting New York City for the 4th of July, 1837

Eight pigs carried by Christopher Columbus to the West Indies were ancestors of animals taken by explorers and the Conquistadores to Mexico, Florida, and New Mexico. "From the increase of these eight pigs have come the pigs found everywhere today in the lands of the Indies, all which ever were there and ever will be, which have been and still are endless."

—Quote from BARTOLOME LAS CASAS,
    missionary-historian of the discovery of America

Boar hunt from Jacques du Fouiloux, 1537. Woodcut.

The Bettmann Archive

INTRODUCTION

The humble porker occupies a special, if somewhat maligned, place in American culture. Its legendary size and appetite have become symbols of disorder and excess: what a pigsty, fat as a pig! But our outward disdain for this lowly beast—in a pig's eye, gone to pigs and whistles, pork barrel politics, you can't make a silk purse from a sow's ear, hogwash, male chauvinist pig, scraping the bottom of the [pork] barrel—belies a deeper, almost childlike affection for things porcine: the three little pigs, pigs in blankets, pigtails, Miss Piggy, porkpie hats, Porky the Pig, and the local Piggly Wiggly convenience store, to name just a few.

The extent to which the pig's image has penetrated our language and popular culture, in song, visual arts, politics, television, and literature, is a reflection of its importance in our development as a nation and as a people. Indeed, it has been said of America that ". . . her railways [were] laid, her canals dug, her ships kept at sea on a porcine diet," and that most Americans ate "fat bacon and pork, fat bacon and pork only, and that continually, morning, noon, and night, for all classes, sexes, ages, and conditions"—a fact difficult to believe in our cholesterol-conscious era. Kentucky was the "Land of Pork and Whisky," Florida, the "Land of Pork and Hominy," and Cincinnati, Ohio, "Porkopolis." A journalist writing in 1845 said: "The putting up of pork has been so important a branch of business in our city for five and twenty years as to have constituted its largest item of manufacture, and acquired for it the sobriquet of Porkopolis. . . . Our pork business is the largest in the world, not even excepting Cork or Belfast in Ireland."

Throughout the pages of *Hog Wild!* you will learn how vital a role the pig played in the fortunes of Americans from every conceivable walk of life: from slave to robber baron, entrepreneur to poet. And through illustrations you will see how the lowly pig, immortalized by old masters and pop icons alike, has captivated our imagination over the centuries.

Hog Wild! has been conceived not merely to pay homage in words and pictures to the animal more American than apple pie itself, but as a showcase for pork cookery as it evolved from colonial times to the present, in all of its diverse ethnic and regional styles.

A visitor to Colima, California, in 1849 described the following scene: "Negroes from the Southern States, mulattoes from Jamaica trudging arm-in-arm with the swarthier Mexicans; Frenchmen, Germans and Italians fraternizing with one another and with the Cockney fresh from the purlieus of St. Giles; an Irishman . . . tracing relationship with the ragged Australian; a few Celestials [Chinese] scattered here and there, their pigtails and conical hats; last of all, a few Indians, the only indigent creatures among all these exotics, lost, swallowed up—out of place." But none of these ethnic groups will be out of place in *Hog Wild!* For all of them and the multitude of others who have since arrived—from Eastern Europe, Asia, South America, and the Caribbean—have contributed to our great American culinary traditions by adapting their native ingredients and cooking styles to the American marketplace. These dishes from faraway places almost always incorporate pork, which, in one form or another, blends beautifully with an international array of seasonings.

Pork can accommodate a diverse range of flavors and spices at a relatively inexpensive price. But its versatility does not end there. It also lends itself to a wide range of cooking methods and a variety of presentations: from casual and hearty one-dish meals suitable for a family gathering; to standing and rolled roasts and sauced medallions for an elegant dinner party; to quick and easy stir-fry and sautéed dishes for the working weekday cook. More to the point, it tastes great. Honestly, admit it. Few things rival a sizzling plate of barbecued ribs or a succulent pork roast with potato pancakes and homemade applesauce.

There is even good news for those closet porkaholics who have restricted their intake of pork for health reasons and for those concerned with reducing dietary fat. America's pork producers, in response to consumer demands, continue in their efforts to breed leaner, meaner meat hogs containing less fat and more protein than before. It is estimated that, on the average, today's pork is 31 percent lower in fat than it was just seven years ago.

Despite its obvious virtues, nobody is suggesting that the "new pork" be incorporated into a daily diet like our forebears'. However, there is nothing wrong with indulging in pork and even other no-nos like butter and cream within a balanced diet accompanied by a healthy exercise routine. So, on those special occasions or on days when the plain broiled fish and naked baked potato just won't do, indulge yourself. Feel free to eat high on the hog, pig out, go whole hog, go *Hog Wild!*

Four pigs (which multiplied to sixty within eighteen months) were among the few survivors of the transatlantic voyage from England to Jamestown made in 1608.

◆

Why are footballs, generally made from cowhide, often referred to as "pigskins"? Because in Jamestown settlement, the ball used to play the game that eventually evolved into contemporary football was an inflated pig's bladder.

◆

The hog census of Massachusetts in 1635 listed the number of pigs as "innumerable."

◆

The Dutch door was invented by New Yorkers (living defensively even in the seventeenth century) to keep out pigs while letting in fresh air.

◆

Colonists smoked pork by hanging hams or sausages in the fireplace chimneys of their kitchens.

◆

Early settlers used "everything but the squeal" of the pig: the pig's meat, head, feet, and jowls for food; its bristles for brushes; its tallow for candles and cooking and lamp oil; its skin for clothing; its blood and innards for puddings; and they even blew up the pig's bladder to make a balloon-type toy or rattle (with the addition of dried peas or beans) for children.

◆

Pigs living in colonial times were so prolific they ran "hog wild" in marauding bands through the streets and fields of settlements from Massachusetts to Virginia, not only vandalizing property but creating diplomatic problems with local Indian tribes.

◆

In the staid and venerable towns of Newport and Boston colonial settlers employed hog catchers to herd strays into pounds.

"The troublesomest old Sow of the Lot"

The Order of the Golden Grease

TURNING ON THE HEAT

"Of all the delicacies in the whole edible world, I will maintain it to be the most delicate of things eaten with bread. . . . There is no flavour comparable, I will contend, to that of the crisp, tawny, well-watched, not over roasted, crackling, as it is well called . . . the fat and lean so blended and running into each other that both together make but one ambrosian result . . ."

—CHARLES LAMB,
"A Dissertation Upon Roast Pig"

Most people I talk to, recounting dinners of shriveled chops, jaw-breaker ribs, and flavorless roasts, contend that they have never had a properly cooked pork dish. They certainly do not wax rhapsodic over roast pork the way Charles Lamb does in the above quotation.

While there is no one technique that magically produces juicy, succulent cooked pork, there are a few important factors you should remember about pork cookery, and meat cookery in general, in order to achieve delicious results with different cuts of pork and various cooking methods.

Heat, whether produced in your oven or your frying pan, can be both friend and foe in meat cookery. Adequate cooking time ensures that certain harmful germs and bacteria are destroyed and that the meat is more palatable. But too much of a proverbial good thing can be bad.

Probably *the* worst, most common mistake people make with pork is to overcook it—for too long a period of time at too high a temperature. This is usually done in an attempt to kill trichinae parasites, a type of nematode worm that can infect hog meat and cause the debilitating and sometimes fatal disease, trichinosis. While parasitic infestation was a common problem before the nineteenth century, the advent of better inspection and breeding conditions for animals has virtually eliminated its incidence. Nonetheless, the fear of trichinosis persists today.

Trichinae and most food-borne bacteria are killed when meat is cooked to an internal temperature of between 137 and 140 degrees Fahrenheit. Yet, the Food and Drug Administration's Safe Cooking Guidelines, erring on the side of caution, still recommend that pork be cooked to an internal temperature of 170 degrees Fahrenheit. Be forewarned! If, acting on your fear of creepy crawly things, you cook a roast until a meat thermometer registers 170 degrees Fahrenheit, by the time you serve it, it will be as palatable as shoe leather.

The National Pork Producers Council advises that pork be cooked to medium doneness, defined as an internal temperature of 160 degrees Fahrenheit. Most contemporary cooks also suggest that pork, particularly leaner cuts, be cooked to medium doneness. However, in this instance, depending upon who is speaking, "medium" is reached when a meat thermometer inserted at the meat's thickest part registers between 145 and 160 degrees Fahrenheit. You also should remember that food continues to cook, and its internal temperature to rise, for *at least* ten minutes after it has been removed from the oven or stove and account for this in approximating cooking and serving time. For example, when cooking a loin or roast, allow the temperature to reach 145 degrees Fahrenheit. Remove the meat from the oven, cover it, and let it rest to settle the juices for ten to twenty minutes. It will finish cooking to around 155 to 160 degrees Fahrenheit during this rest time. Or, if you are preparing cuts that require a quick saucing, let the internal temperature register 155 degrees Fahrenheit, then plate and serve them immediately.

If you are cooking without a meat thermometer—for example, making a stew or broiling chops—there are other ways to determine the degree of doneness:

- By touch. Stick the tip of a sharp kitchen knife into the thickest part of the meat and hold it there for ten seconds. Remove the knife tip and *carefully* touch it to your lower lip. How does it feel? Cool or cold to the touch indicates rare, warm indicates medium, and hot means you probably overcooked it.

- By feel. Rare meat feels soft and yields to pressure. To get an idea, relax and dangle your hand. Then feel the skin between your thumb and index finger. This is "rare meat." Medium-done meat has more firmness. Stretch your hand, tense your fingers, and feel the area between your thumb and first finger. This is the feel of medium. Well-done meat is hard and unyielding and feels much like the tip of your nose. This method is preferred by many restaurant chefs and professional cooks for both aesthetic and practical reasons: The meat has no ugly cuts or poke holes from which juices can escape, and therefore looks and tastes better upon final presentation. The only disadvantage to this method is the time and practice it takes to master.

- By sight. You can use this same technique on chicken. Prick the meat with a knife and examine the color of the juices bubbling up. If red or rosy in color, the meat is not quite done. If the juices are clear or golden colored, the meat is cooked. If there are no juices at all, you have a problem.

If none of the above techniques appeals to you, there is still another tried-and-true method. Cut into the meat and look at it. Friends and family will forgive this transgression if it means the difference between perfectly cooked versus undercooked meat. If the pork is slightly pink in the center and uniformly white/gray throughout, the meat is done. Certain cuts may be a darker brown or pink color near the bone. This is perfectly normal. Cured meats will be bright pink to red in color rather than white.

The amount of cooking time needed will vary depending upon the size and cut of the meat. (See the table on page 10 for general cooking times.) Obviously, smaller or thinner pieces of meat will cook more quickly than larger ones. But as far as meat is concerned, all things are not equal. Do not assume that a five-pound boned loin roast (enough to feed twelve to fourteen people) requires the same cooking time as a five-pound boned sirloin roast (feeds six to eight persons) or ham (enough for eight to ten people). Whereas 1 to 1½ hours in the oven would probably suffice for a loin, the sirloin roast or ham might require twice that cooking time. In part, this is due to the physical qualities of the various cuts, which come from different parts of the animal.

The pig is divided into five major sections, each with distinct taste and textural characteristics:

1. The shoulder, or Boston shoulder. Different "Boston" cuts include boneless and bone-in blade roasts, blade steaks, and pork cubes. Like other cuts coming from a part of the animal that moves about a great deal and has a large amount of connective tissue, e.g., the leg, butt, or neck, shoulder cuts tend to be fattier and more flavorful but tougher. They

benefit from a longer, slower cooking method like braising (cooking partially immersed in liquid, with "wet heat") or roasting at low temperatures (with indirect "dry heat"). Smaller cuts, like cubes for shish kebab or ground pork burgers, may be cooked with a direct heat method such as grilling or broiling.

2. The picnic shoulder, cut from the foreleg. Picnic shoulders are primarily cut into hams, either to be cooked fresh (braised or roasted) or smoked.

3. The loin, which extends along the back from the shoulder to the hip. It includes back and baby back ribs; Canadian bacon; rib, loin, and sirloin chops; boneless loin roasts; the tenderloin; and blade, center, and sirloin roasts (bone-in). The blade chops or roasts come from the section of the loin closest to the shoulder; center cuts, from the central portion; and sirloin roasts from the hindmost section near the rump or butt. Meat from the loin section is generally the leanest and tenderest of all, and can be used in a variety of ways. Thinner cuts, like chops, fillets, or cutlets, benefit from quick direct heat cooking methods like panfrying, sautéing, broiling, or grilling, while larger cuts are usually roasted or braised. Because of its lower fat content and relatively quick cooking time, extra care must be taken to prevent dryness when preparing loin cuts. Make sure to leave a thin layer of fat on the meat. You may even wish to coat the meat lightly with oil before broiling, grilling, or roasting. When panfrying or sautéing, make sure the pan is well coated with oil or fat. Basting with fat or leftover marinade will also help produce a moister roast.

4. The leg (hind). From this section we get fresh hams, boned and bone-in; rump or butt portion hams (from the upper leg); shank portion hams (from the lower leg); and ham steaks. The larger cuts should be roasted or braised. Fresh,

uncured ham may be roasted whole or sliced thinly for stir-frying, sautéing, or grilling. Cured ham steaks or slices simply require reheating.

5. The belly, which yields spareribs, slab and sliced bacon, salt pork, and sow's belly. With the exception of spareribs, most belly parts, due to their high fat content, will be used as flavoring or moisturizing ingredients in recipes.

Other factors—in addition to cooking time and technique and the type of cut—will help contribute to a moister result when using pork, namely, your preparation of the meat prior to cooking it.

A marinade, comprising an acid (e.g., citrus juice, vinegar, wine), an oil, and flavoring ingredients, will enhance the taste and improve the texture of the meat. The acid will help tenderize tough fibers, while the oil will help lubricate the meat and protect it from dryness. Always marinate in a nonreactive glass, enamel, or plastic container (as opposed to copper or aluminum, which will have a chemical reaction with the marinade acid) for up to two hours at room temperature or for several hours refrigerated. You can mix the marinade early in the morning, add it to the meat before leaving for work, cover and refrigerate, and prepare it that evening. The longer the meat marinates, the more flavorful it will be.

Curing with salt, a more time-consuming process, is another method that tenderizes and preserves meat. Most commonly used in combination with smoking for larger cuts like hams, both wet and dry curing can be employed with smaller cuts as well. However, you should be aware that salt, like heat, can become a deadly weapon if abused. As a preservative, salt breaks down proteins, concentrates fat, and extrudes from the meat fluids that would cause it to decay under normal circumstances. Because of this last factor, *never* sprinkle salt directly onto a piece of unlubricated pork prior to cooking. It will draw out the meat's natural juices and result in dryness. Only salt meat after it has been coated with some type of oil or fat.

These techniques and others will be discussed in greater detail in the following recipes, arranged by cooking methodology and using a variety of appropriate cuts.

The following is a chart showing average serving sizes and cooking times for various pork products. All figures are for four servings, unless otherwise indicated. Specific cooking methodologies and temperatures appear with individual recipes. This is for use as a general guideline for purchasing and timing allocations.

GENERAL COOKING TIMES

Type of Meat	Amount Used	Serving per Person	Approximate Cooking Time
Boneless Loin Cutlets, ¼ inch	1 pound	¼ pound	2 minutes/side
Boneless Loin Medallions	1½ pounds	2 3-ounce medallions	3–4 minutes/side
Loin Chops, ½ inch	8 chops	2 chops	4–5 minutes/side
Loin Chops, 1–1¼ inch	4 chops	1 chop (8–10 ounces)	7–8 minutes/side
Ribs, Baby Back	4 pounds	1 pound (1 "rack")	15 minutes
Ribs, Country	4 pounds	1 pound (3 ribs)	25 minutes
Spareribs	5–6 pounds (serves 4–6)	1–1½ pounds (¾–1 rack each)	1½–2 hours
Roast, Loin, Boneless	2–3 pounds (serves 4–6)	6–8 ounces	1–1¼ hours
Roast, Loin, Butterflied, Stuffed	2–3 pounds (serves 4–6)	6–8 ounces	45 minutes–1 hour

◆

GENERAL COOKING TIMES

Type of Meat	Amount Used	Serving per Person	Approximate Cooking Time
Roast, Tenderloin	1–1¼ pounds	5–6 ounces	20–25 minutes
Roast, Crown Rib	8 pounds (serves 8)	1 pound	2 hours
Sausages, 3–4 inch	1½–2 pounds	3 sausages	10 minutes
Sausages, 5–6 inch	2–2⅓ pounds	2 sausages	10–15 minutes
Stew Meat, butt or shoulder cubes	1½ pounds	6 ounces	1¼–1½ hours
Ham Steak, Cooked	1½–2 pounds	Half a steak	5–7 minutes
Ham, Fresh (half)	7–8 pounds (serves 8)	1 pound	2–2½ hours
Ham, Fresh (whole)	14–16 pounds (serves 16–20)	12–14 ounces	3–3½ hours
Ham, Cured (whole)	14–16 pounds (serves 16)	12–14 ounces	up to 6 hours

Pig pickin' and politickin' is an old Southern custom. While campaigning in their districts before election time, candidates would sponsor big barbecues on the local courthouse square for all their constituents. George Washington's expenditures when he ran for the Virginia Burgess were between £25 and £50, several times the price of the house and parcel of land one needed to own to qualify as a voter.

◆

Thomas Jefferson is often remembered for, among many things, his appreciation of fine foods and wines. During his tenure as governor of Virginia, his culinary style was severely cramped when the British, waging battle in the Revolutionary War, destroyed his cherished food stores and wine cellars and interrupted regular commerce. This forced him to acquire substandard foodstuffs at exorbitant prices far afield from Monticello. To compensate for his losses, both culinary and monetary, he instructed his agents to intercept hogs being driven to market in Richmond and buy them all. He then resold them at inflated prices to local butchers, who, expressing their feelings about the Jefferson hog monopoly, draped pig entrails all along the fences surrounding his house and referred to him only as "the Hog Governor" for many years afterward.

◆

Mary Terhune, a nineteenth-century cookbook writer, claimed: ". . . seeing how pigs live, one cannot marvel at the growing prejudice against pork in all its varieties."

◆

The typical nineteenth-century American breakfast, "no evanescent thing," comprised ham, beef, sausages, pork, bread, butter, boiled potatoes, pies, coffee, and cider. Average calorie consumption was 4,000 calories per day.

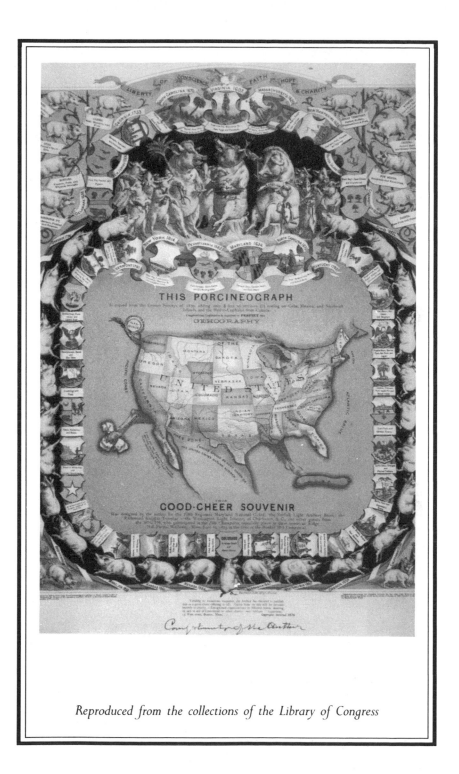

SOUPS
AND APPETIZERS

"Meals were pork upon pork and again pork upon that. . . . These people live so much upon the swine's flesh that it doesn't only incline them to yaws and consequently to the downfall of their noses, but makes them likewise extremely hoggish in their temper and many of them seem to grunt rather than speak in their ordinary conversation."

—WILLIAM BYRD, a Virginia planter, regarding the people of North Carolina in the early 1700s

In the age of the all-porcine diet, appetizers using pork were probably commonplace. Nowhere is pork's diversity better showcased than in this group of recipes. Highlighting the meat in its myriad forms—cubed and ground; cured and fresh; made into bacon, ham, and sausages—this section includes recipes for soups, salads, and hot hors d'oeuvres.

Other recipes appearing later in the book would be appropriate to serve as appetizers as well, for example, the Southwestern Quiche (page 68), the Empanadas (page 66), or the Pig Balls Stroganoff (page 90). Just adjust the portions according to the number of people being served.

Perhaps the most important recipe in the section is the one for pork stock. A good rich stock can serve as the basis for any number of dishes—soups, sauces, gravies, a braising liquid to add extra flavor.

James Beard, dean of American cookery, suggested that chicken stocks needed a little pork in them to achieve peak flavor. Here, the addition of pork bones and spices to what is basically a chicken stock can transform the mundane into something more special.

Straight or frozen as meat glaze (*glace de viande*, page 188), pork stock is especially good when used with pork recipes. While chicken or even beef stock can serve as an emergency stand-in, pork stock really is preferable. Beef stock overpowers the more delicate taste of pork whereas the pork stock adds that *je ne sais quoi* chicken broth lacks. Another plus: You can easily use the pork stock in chicken recipes or for your Thanksgiving turkey gravy. It is, like most other pork products, versatile.

Courtesy of the New York Historical Society, New York City

To limit the rampages of free-range pigs in their grain fields Manhattan Islanders erected a long permanent wall along the northern edge of their settlement—the eponymous Wall Street—where, in 1641 "the slaughter-houses and cattle pens were almost as conspicuous on the landscape as windmills in Holland." The packing district was subsequently moved from beyond Wall Street to more spacious quarters on present-day Pearl Street between Wall and Pine, where some 4,000 cattle and a larger number of hogs were slaughtered each year.

PORK STOCK

This stock can be used as a stock base or clarified for broth. If you're planning to cook a pork roast, it makes terrific use of those unwanted bones. Ask the butcher to save them for you or try boning the roast yourself. Experiment by adding other types of bones to the stockpot— e.g., from duck or veal—for an even richer, more complex-tasting soup. Quantities can be increased.

Bones from a sirloin pork roast or other nonfatty cut
Backs and wings from 2 to 3 chickens
2 stalks celery
1 large onion
2 carrots
3 garlic cloves, peeled and left whole
4 juniper berries
2 allspice berries
2 cloves
10 black peppercorns
Bouquet garni (thyme, parsley, and bay leaf)
2 tablespoons tomato paste

Place the bones in a large pan and cover them with cold water. Bring the water to a boil and reduce it to a simmer. Skim the brown scum from the surface as it appears, removing as much as possible, and add all the remaining ingredients to the stockpot. Continue to skim the surface as necessary. Simmer the stock for 2 to 3 hours.

Strain the stock through a China cap (see note) or other strainer lined with cheesecloth, pressing on the solids to extract all the juices. Cool the stock immediately in an ice bath, uncovered.

If you plan to use the stock for sauce, reduce it by half to concentrate its flavor.

Yield: 4 to 6 cups

NOTE: A fine-meshed strainer used for sauces.

.:.

GINGERED PORK CONSOMMÉ

6 cups Pork Stock (page 18)
¼ cup julienned fresh ginger
3 egg whites, lightly beaten
2 tablespoons chopped fresh coriander (cilantro)

Bring the stock to a boil in a large saucepan over high heat. Add the julienned fresh ginger, reduce the heat, and simmer the stock for half an hour.

To clarify the stock for consommé: Remove as much surface grease from the stock as possible. Whisk a few ladles of hot stock into the egg whites. Add the egg whites to the stockpot in a thin stream, whisking continuously, until the stock returns to a simmer. Stop whisking and pull the pan halfway off to the side of the burner. At this point the egg whites will have solidified to make a "raft," which traps the impurities and clarifies the stock. Carefully make a hole in the side of the raft located over the burner. The soup will simmer through this hole and over the raft. Let the stock simmer, *undisturbed*, for 10 minutes. Strain *very carefully* through a China cap lined with cheesecloth or through a strainer lined with a coffee filter. The broth should be very clear and grease-free.

Garnish the soup with the chopped coriander.

Yield: 4 servings

HAWG 'N' HOMINY

This dish, often called posole, *is a traditional Southwestern offering at Christmastime or the New Year. It can be served either as a soup or as a side dish that perfectly complements New Mexican, Tex-Mex, or other dishes of the region like enchiladas.*

2 tablespoons vegetable oil
¾ pound pork ribs or other bony, fatty cut (e.g., neck bones)
1 medium onion, chopped
2 ears fresh corn
1 pig's foot, split
6 cups water or Pork Stock (page 18)
2 teaspoons chili paste (such as sambal oelek or a New Mexican chili paste), more or less to taste
2 large garlic cloves, minced
1 30-ounce can white hominy, drained

Heat the oil in a large heavy casserole or soup pot over medium-high heat. Add the ribs and sauté them on all sides until they are nicely browned. Remove them from the pot and set them aside.

Add the onion to the casserole and cook it over medium heat

until soft and translucent. While the onion is cooking, cut the kernels from the corn and set them aside. Discard the cobs.

Add the reserved ribs or bones, pig's foot, and stock to the casserole and bring the mixture to a boil. Lower the heat to a simmer and skim off any foam or scum rising to the surface.

Add all the remaining ingredients to the *posole* and simmer it, uncovered, for 2½ to 3 hours, or until it reaches the desired consistency. (For soup, cook the *posole* 2½ hours. For a side dish, cook the *posole* longer, or until almost all the water has evaporated.) Remove the pig's foot and bones from the soup. Chop any of the meat from the bones and add it to the *posole*.

Yield: 4 servings

HOPPIN' JOHN

Hog meat is a symbol of success in certain areas of the country. Black-eyed peas served with hog jowls is a traditional New Year's Day feast down south. The peas symbolize money and the hog jowls are for good luck. Often, a coin would be buried in the dish of peas and the person who found it in his or her bowl would be assured good luck for the year. This recipe dispenses with the hog jowls, replaced here with a smoked ham hock.

½ *pound black-eyed peas, rinsed and picked over*
1 *pound andouille sausage or kielbasa, sliced into* ¼*-inch rounds*
1 *large onion, minced*
2 *stalks celery, minced*

1 green pepper, minced
1 ham hock
1 tablespoon tomato paste
2 bay leaves
2 small garlic cloves, minced
½ teaspoon dried thyme
½ teaspoon dried basil
½ teaspoon black pepper
1 teaspoon dried red pepper flakes (more or less, to taste)
Salt and pepper
Cooked rice
Tabasco sauce

Place the peas in a medium saucepan with enough water to cover them by two inches. Bring the peas to a boil over high heat, and boil them for 2 minutes. Remove the peas from the heat and allow them to stand, covered, for 2 hours.

Sauté the andouille sausage in a skillet over medium heat until it is nicely browned. Remove the sausage slices with a slotted spoon and set them aside. Sauté the onion, celery, and pepper in the sausage fat over medium heat until they are golden and translucent.

Drain the peas and place them in a kettle with 3½ cups pea soaking liquid plus water. Add all the remaining ingredients except for the rice and Tabasco sauce to the peas. Bring the peas to a boil. Reduce the heat to low and simmer the peas, uncovered, for 1½ to 2 hours, or until the peas are tender and the liquid is slightly thickened. Season the peas with salt and pepper to taste.

Serve the Hoppin' John with cooked rice and Tabasco.

Yield: 4 servings

MOORS AND CHRISTIANS

Here's a dish hailing from Florida, also known as black bean soup with rice. The rather unusual name, recalling Florida's history of Spanish settlement, harks back to a less gentle era in Spanish history during which the forces of the black "infidels," in this case, beans, waged battle with the forces of the white and "righteous," represented by steamed rice. Serve with minced onion, vinegar, chopped fresh green pepper, and cheddar cheese, if desired.

½ **pound black beans**
6 **cups water**
2 **tablespoons butter**
1 **large red onion, cut up**
3 **celery stalks, sliced**
1 **ham hock**
1¼**-pound piece of ham**
3 **garlic cloves**
2 **teaspoons ground cumin**
2 **large slices orange peel**
2 **bay leaves**
6 **stalks fresh coriander (cilantro)**
6 **black peppercorns**
1 **teaspoon dried** epazote *(see note)*
Salt
Black pepper
¼ **teaspoon cayenne pepper**

Rinse the beans and pick them over. Bring them to a boil in a medium saucepan with 6 cups water. Boil the beans for 2 minutes and remove them from the heat. Let the beans soak, covered, for at least 2 hours.

Melt the butter in a large soup pot over medium heat. Add the onion and celery and sauté them, covered, until they are softened, about 10 minutes. Drain the beans but reserve their soaking liquid. Add the beans, ham hock, ham, garlic, and cumin, and the orange peel, bay leaves, cilantro, and peppercorns wrapped and tied in a small piece of cheesecloth to the onion and celery mixture. Add enough of the soaking liquid and additional water, if necessary, to cover the ingredients completely. Bring the soup to a boil. Reduce the heat and simmer the soup, uncovered, for 2 hours, or until the beans are tender. Remove the soup from the heat. Let it cool and refrigerate overnight.

Before serving, remove the ham, ham hock, and cheesecloth bag from the soup. Pass half of the soup through the fine blade of a food mill. Chop or grind the ham up with the soup. Add the *epazote*, salt, black pepper, cayenne pepper, and additional cumin and chopped cilantro to taste.

Yield: 4 servings

NOTE: A dried herb available in Latin specialty stores.

NEW ENGLAND CLAM CHOWDER

New Englanders traditionally used pork as a flavoring in food rather than as an ingredient per se. A truly authentic New England clam chowder must be flavored and garnished with salt pork cracklings.

3 dozen clams
2 tablespoons dry vermouth
3 ounces salt pork, cut into ¼-inch dice

1 stalk celery, cut into ¼-inch dice
2 small carrots, cut into ¼-inch dice
1 medium onion, finely minced
2 tablespoons flour
1 pound white potatoes, peeled and cut into ¼-inch dice
1 bay leaf
¼ teaspoon dried thyme
½ cup heavy cream
½ cup milk
Salt and pepper

Scrub the clams and rinse them in three changes of cold water. Place the clams in a large pot with an inch of water and the vermouth. Cover and steam the clams over medium heat until they just begin to open. Reserve the liquid used to steam the clams. Pry open the shells and remove the clam meat, being careful to reserve all of their liquid. Strain the clam juice into a measuring cup and reserve enough steaming liquid to make 3 cups. Chop the clams and refrigerate them.

Sauté the salt pork in a small sauté pan until nicely browned and crisp. Drain the cracklings on paper towels and reserve 2 tablespoons rendered fat. Sauté the celery, carrots, and onions in the pork fat over medium heat until they are softened and translucent, 8 to 10 minutes. Add the flour to the vegetables all at once, and stir constantly over high heat for 3 to 4 minutes, or until the flour turns golden. Add the 3 cups reserved clam liquid, the potatoes, bay leaf, and thyme. Simmer the soup for 15 to 20 minutes, or until the potatoes are tender. Add the clams and simmer for an additional 10 minutes. Add the cream and milk. Season with salt and pepper. Garnish with the cracklings.

Yield: 4 servings

PORTUGUESE SOUP

Portuguese immigrants settled in seaport towns along the east coast of the United States, for example, in Connecticut and Massachusetts. This recipe uses linguiça, a spicy Portuguese sausage similar to pepperoni but with the addition of vinegar, spices, and liquid smoke. Other vegetables and types of beans, such as cabbage and chick-peas, can be added or substituted in the soup. Just make sure that the vegetables are cut into a very small dice.

1½ pounds kale, stemmed and rinsed
2 tablespoons butter
2 stalks celery, cut into ¼-inch dice
1 large onion, minced
3 small (or 1 very large) leeks, cut into ¼-inch slices
2 carrots, cut into ¼-inch dice
1 pound linguiça sausage, cut into ¼-inch slices
1 pound white potatoes, peeled and cut into ¼-inch dice
2 cups dry, light-bodied red wine, such as Rioja
5 cups water
1 large bay leaf
½ teaspoon black pepper
½ teaspoon dried thyme
¼ teaspoon cayenne pepper
1½ teaspoons salt
1 1-pound can red kidney beans, drained

Add the kale in batches to the bowl of a food processor fitted with a steel blade. Process the kale until it is finely chopped, and set it aside.

Melt the butter in a large soup pot over medium heat. Add the celery, onion, leek, and carrots and cook them, covered, until the vegetables are softened, approximately 10 to 15 minutes. Add the sausages and sauté them for 5 minutes, or until they are cooked through. Add all of the remaining ingredients. Bring the soup to a boil. Lower the heat and simmer the soup, uncovered, for 2 hours. Adjust the soup for seasonings. Serve piping hot.

Yield: 4 servings

·:·

THREE-BEAN SOUP WITH BACON

Here is a variation on a classical soup of white beans flavored with bacon.

½ cup dried navy beans
½ cup dried baby lima beans
½ cup dried yellow split peas
6 cups water
3 small carrots
2 celery stalks
1 large onion
1 turnip
6 ounces sliced bacon, cut into ¼ X 1-inch strips
1 bay leaf
½ teaspoon dried thyme or 2 sprigs fresh
6 sprigs flat-leaf parsley
4 fresh or dried sage leaves
12 black peppercorns
Salt and pepper

Rinse off the beans and remove any foreign particles from them. Place the beans in a medium saucepan with 6 cups water and bring them to a boil for 2 minutes. Remove the beans from the heat and let them soak, covered, for 2 hours.

Cut up the vegetables into small pieces and set them aside. (They do not have to be cut neatly because the soup will be pureed at the end of its cooking.) Sauté the bacon strips in a large soup pot or Dutch oven over medium heat until they begin to render their fat and turn golden. Do not let them brown. Add the vegetables and sauté them, covered, over low heat, until softened, about 15 to 20 minutes.

Drain the beans and reserve their soaking liquid. Add the beans, 4 cups reserved soaking liquid, the herbs, and the spices to the vegetable mixture. Simmer, uncovered, for 1½ hours, or until the beans are tender.

Pass the soup through the fine blade of a food mill or puree the mixture using a hand-held blender. Season with salt and pepper to taste.

Yield: 4 servings

BACON CHEDDAR CRACKERS

These crackers are especially good served with cream cheese.

⅓ pound bacon
⅔ cup all-purpose flour
⅓ cup rye flour
¼ cup wheat germ
1 teaspoon baking soda
½ teaspoon salt
½ teaspoon white pepper
2 ounces cheddar cheese, grated (approximately 1 cup)

1 teaspoon caraway seed
½ cup plain unsweetened yogurt
2 tablespoons mustard

Preheat the oven to 350° F.

Cook the bacon in a sauté pan over medium heat until it is crisp. Drain the cooked bacon on paper towels and reserve 2 tablespoons bacon fat.

Combine the flours, wheat germ, baking soda, salt, and pepper in the container of a food processor and pulse a few times to combine the ingredients. Add the cooked bacon and pulse it until the mixture is crumbly and the bacon is uniformly distributed. Add the cheddar cheese and caraway seed and pulse to combine. Mix the reserved bacon fat with the yogurt and mustard. With the motor running, add the liquid gradually in a thin stream until the dough forms a ball. (You may not need to add all of the yogurt to the dough.)

Remove the dough from the food processor and roll it out on a lightly floured surface to ⅛-inch thickness. With a cookie cutter or knife, cut the dough into 1¾-inch squares. Place the squares on an ungreased baking sheet and bake them for 15 to 18 minutes, or until nicely browned.

Yield: 4 dozen crackers

BLT SALAD DRESSING

Here is that old standby, the bacon, lettuce, and tomato sandwich with mayonnaise, with a new twist. For best results, use only very ripe and flavorful tomatoes.

10 ounces ripe red tomatoes
¼ pound bacon
2 large iceberg lettuce leaves
½ cup mayonnaise
2 tablespoons ketchup
Salt and pepper
½ tablespoon pickle relish (optional)

Drop the tomatoes into a pan of boiling water for 10 to 15 seconds. Drain and refresh them under cold water. Peel (the skins should slip off easily), core, and cut the tomatoes in half and squeeze out the seeds into a small sieve placed over a bowl to catch the juices. Reserve the tomato juice and discard the seeds.

Fry the bacon in a sauté pan over medium heat until it is crisp, being careful not to burn it. Drain the cooked bacon on paper towels and cool it to room temperature.

Place the bacon strips in the container of a blender or food processor. Pulse it a few times to break up the bacon into smaller pieces. Add the tomatoes, tomato juice, and remaining ingredients and puree the dressing until it is well blended but still retains some crunchy bits. Chill the dressing for several hours in the refrigerator.

Yield: Approximately 2 cups

GREENS WITH GOAT CHEESE AND WARM BACON VINAIGRETTE

This salad is not for the cholesterol-conscious. The warm vinaigrette, made with hot bacon fat, would go nicely with regular salad greens or with a spinach salad as well. If you really want to go overboard, you can crumble or slice the bacon to go on top of the salad. Just make sure to sauté the bacon at the last minute so the vinaigrette remains warm.

Vegetable oil
2 cups 1-inch-square white bread cubes
2 garlic cloves, peeled and cut in half
⅓ pound thick-cut bacon (approximately 4 slices)
1 tablespoon Dijon mustard
2 tablespoons red wine vinegar
6 tablespoons safflower oil
Salt and pepper to taste
8 cups frisee or other mixed salad greens, washed and dried
      thoroughly
4 ounces chèvre or other mild-tasting goat cheese, divided
      into 4 portions

Special equipment: 1 large brown paper bag

Heat one-half inch of vegetable oil in a frying pan over high heat. When it reaches 350°F., drop the bread cubes into the hot oil and fry them until they are golden brown. Be careful not to burn the bread. It will cook very quickly, in only seconds. Place the croutons in the brown paper bag with the garlic. Shake the croutons in the bag to help degrease them and to flavor them with the garlic.

Sauté the bacon in a frying pan over medium heat. While the bacon is cooking, mix together the mustard and vinegar in a small bowl. Whisk in the safflower oil gradually to form an emulsified sauce. Reserve 6 tablespoons of rendered bacon fat and, while still hot, whisk the fat into the vinaigrette and season it with salt and pepper to taste.

Toss the salad greens with the warm vinaigrette in a large salad or mixing bowl. Divide the greens among four salad or serving plates. Top each serving with a portion of the goat cheese, croutons, and bacon pieces, if desired. Serve the salad immediately.

Yield: 4 servings

CHINESE RAVIOLI IN SESAME SAUCE

1 recipe Pork Quenelles (page 38)
30 wonton wrappers
1 tablespoon minced ginger
2 small garlic cloves, minced
½ cup sesame paste (tahini)
2 tablespoons soy sauce
2 tablespoons sesame oil
¼ cup water
2 tablespoons rice wine vinegar
1 small carrot, finely julienned
1 small stalk celery, finely julienned

Place 2 level teaspoons meat filling in the center of a wonton wrapper. Moisten the edges with water. Place another wonton skin on top of the filling and press the edges together to seal them tightly. Place the finished ravioli under a piece of plastic wrap while you proceed with the rest. Repeat this process. (You may have some wonton wrappers left over.)

Combine the ginger, garlic, sesame paste, soy sauce, sesame oil, water, and rice wine vinegar, and stir to combine the ingredients thoroughly. Keep the sauce covered.

To cook the ravioli: Bring a large pot of salted water to a boil. Reduce the heat to a simmer. Drop the raviolis into the water, a few at a time, and stir to prevent them from sticking together. Cook the raviolis until their tops are slightly sunken in and the filling is cooked through, approximately 8 to 10 minutes. Drain the ravioli and toss them together with the sesame sauce. Garnish with the julienne of carrot and celery.

Yield: 4 to 5 servings

·:·

STUFFED CABBAGE ROLLS

A version of this particular dish can be found in the recipe file of just about every cook of Eastern European descent, including Hungarians, Poles, Russians, and Czechs. While there are variations from country to country—some recipes might include a sweet-and-sour sauce, fruit, pork, beef, or a number of different ingredients—one thing is certain: The results are satisfying and delicious.

12 large green cabbage leaves
½ pound ground pork
½ pound ground beef
1 cup cooked white rice

½ cup raisins
1 small onion, finely minced
2 garlic cloves, minced
1 egg
Salt and pepper
Nutmeg
Cayenne pepper
1 pound sauerkraut
1 ham hock

SAUCE

2 tablespoons butter
3 tablespoons flour
1 tablespoon tomato paste
1 teaspoon dill seed
¾ teaspoon paprika
Salt and pepper
1 tablespoon snipped fresh dill weed

Blanch the cabbage leaves, 2 or 3 at a time, in a large kettle of boiling salted water until softened, approximately 3 to 4 minutes. Reserve the cooking liquid.

Combine the ground meats, rice, raisins, onion, garlic, egg, and spices to taste in a medium mixing bowl. (To test for seasoning, sauté a small amount of the meat mixture and adjust the spices accordingly. Remember, you can always add more spice, but you cannot remove it once it's in.) Divide the filling into 12 equal portions.

Place a portion of the filling into the center of a cabbage leaf. Fold the sides and then the top of the cabbage leaf over the ground meat mixture, and roll it up to fully enclose the filling. Repeat with the remaining cabbage leaves and filling.

Place the sauerkraut in a Dutch oven large enough to hold the cabbage rolls in a single layer. Position the ham hock in the center of the pan and arrange the stuffed cabbage on top of the sauerkraut and around the hock. Add enough cabbage cooking liquid to just cover the cabbage rolls; reserve 2 cups of the liquid for the sauce. Bring the liquid to a boil. Lower the heat and simmer the cabbage rolls, covered, for 2 hours.

To prepare the sauce: Make a roux by melting the butter in a saucepan over medium-high heat. Add the flour to the butter all at once, whisking constantly to incorporate it. Still whisking, cook the mixture approximately 3 minutes, or until it is golden in color. Add 2 cups strained cabbage cooking liquid, the tomato paste, dill seed, paprika, and salt and pepper to taste. Lower the heat and whisk until the sauce is thickened. Adjust the seasoning. Add the fresh dill. Serve immediately.

Yield: 6 appetizer or 4 main course servings

·:·

PIGS IN BLANKETS

A truly American cocktail appetizer, the pig in a blanket can inspire love in baby boomers hungry for the food of the 1950s and 1960s and fear and loathing for those uninitiated in the mysteries of "mommy cuisine." These are tasty and delectable morsels, best savored with a bit of nostalgia, lots of flavored mustards, and plenty of napkins.

1 pound puff pastry
2 tablespoons Dijon mustard
Hot Hungarian paprika
½ cup grated Parmesan cheese
20 cocktail frankfurters
1 egg, lightly beaten with 1 tablespoon water

Roll out the dough into a ¼-inch thick rectangle measuring 20 X 10 inches.

Spread the mustard thinly over one-half of the pastry and sprinkle it generously with the paprika and Parmesan cheese. Fold the dough over so that the mustard layer is sealed inside. Roll out the pastry into a 10-inch square and trim any rough edges with a sharp knife.

Cut the dough into 20 smaller 2 X 2½-inch rectangles. Place a cocktail frankfurter along the short edge of each rectangle and roll the dough to enclose the frankfurter. Brush the edge of the dough with a bit of cold water to seal the seam and place the pig in a blanket, seam side down, on a parchment-lined baking sheet. Repeat this process with the remaining rectangles. Chill the pigs in blankets in the refrigerator for 1 hour.

Preheat the oven to 375°F.

Remove the franks from the refrigerator and brush their tops with the beaten egg, being careful not to let the egg wash drip down the edges. Bake the pigs in blankets in the preheated oven 15 to 20 minutes, or until they are puffed and golden. Serve immediately.

Yield: 20 hors d'oeuvres

·:·

PINCHITOS

Hernando de Soto, the Spanish explorer who discovered the Mississippi River in 1541, endured vicious attacks launched by Indians with the purpose of liberating the Spanish hogs for their own culinary purposes. The following recipe is based upon a dish served at festivals and street fairs in Moorish Spain around de Soto's time: marinated skewered meat, wrapped in bread and hot from the brazier, sold to passersby as they enjoyed local festivities. While at their peak flavor when barbecued over hot coals, the pinchitos can be cooked under the broiler as well for a wintertime treat.

1 cup orange juice
¼ cup olive oil
2 teaspoons grated orange rind
1 garlic clove, minced
1 teaspoon each ground coriander, cumin, chili powder,
     black pepper, and hot paprika
½ teaspoon each dried oregano (crushed), turmeric, and salt
1 pound pork, cut into ½-inch cubes
Pita bread

Special equipment: 20 6-inch skewers

Combine the orange juice, oil, orange rind, garlic, herbs, and spices in a nonreactive bowl or container. Add the meat and let it marinate for several hours or overnight in the refrigerator.

About an hour before you plan to cook the pinchitos, remove the meat from the refrigerator and let it stand at room temperature. At the same time, soak the skewers in water.

Prepare a barbecue grill or preheat a broiler.

Thread the meat onto the skewers and cook it, basting with the marinade, approximately 2 to 3 minutes per side. Serve the pinchitos with pita bread.

Yield: 4 servings (5 skewers apiece)

PORK QUENELLES

These quenelles, or meat dumplings, are light, elegant, and easy to prepare. And, unlike traditional quenelles, they contain no heavy cream. When cooked, they are a lovely white—almost indistinguishable from chicken in taste and appearance—flecked with orange and green. Serve them with the Gingered Pork Consommé (page 19), or use the mixture as a filling for Chinese Ravioli in Sesame Sauce (page 32). The meat is ground separately from the other ingredients to give the quenelles some texture.

½ pound lean pork loin, cubed
1 teaspoon grated fresh ginger
1½ teaspoons finely minced onion
4 canned water chestnuts, grated
½ teaspoon salt
1 teaspoon chopped fresh coriander (cilantro)
½ teaspoon grated fresh tangerine rind
1 knifepoint of cinnamon
1 egg
4 cups water or stock for poaching

Pulse the pork cubes in the bowl of a food processor until they are coarsely chopped. Then, process the meat to a very smooth paste. Add the remaining ingredients to the workbowl except for the water or stock, and pulse or stir to blend them in thoroughly.

Form the quenelles: With 2 teaspoons (not measuring spoons), take a spoonful of the meat mixture in one spoon and hold the spoon angled slightly down and away from you. Use the other spoon to scoop the meat in an upward angle toward you. Repeat this process until the quenelle takes on a smooth football shape.

Carefully spoon the finished quenelles onto a heat-proof plate and chill them for approximately ½ hour.

Bring the salted water or the stock to a boil in a wide sauce or sauté pan over high heat. Reduce the heat to a simmer. To loosen the quenelles from the plate and into the pan, ladle a bit of hot liquid over them (they will slide right in). Poach the quenelles for 8 to 10 minutes, or until they are cooked through. (To test for doneness, a knife stuck into the center of a quenelle should feel hot when touched to your lip. If you're not sure, cut into one. It should be uniformly white, not pink, throughout.) When cooked, drain the quenelles on paper towels. The cooked quenelles can be kept 1 to 2 days, refrigerated.

Yield: 4 to 6 appetizer servings

·:·

TERRINE OF RABBIT AND PORK

This terrine, if well covered with fat, will keep in the refrigerator, uncut, for up to two weeks. This will also allow the flavors to mellow, and give the cook some leeway with preparation time.

1 rabbit, approximately 3 pounds
Black pepper
¾ cup cognac
1 pound lean ground pork
½ pound ground veal
1 pound pork fat, ground
1 small onion, minced and sautéed in 1 tablespoon butter
4 small garlic cloves, minced

1 1/2 teaspoons épices fines *(page 93)*
2 to 3 teaspoons salt
1/2 teaspoon black pepper
2 eggs
8 ounces leaf lard for lining the mold
4-ounce piece of ham, julienned
1/2 cup whole toasted hazelnuts

Two to three days before you wish to serve the pâté: Remove the meat from the rabbit with a sharp boning knife. Take approximately half the meat—e.g., the best parts, like the tenderloin—and cut it into thin strips 1/2 inch thick. (The other half, comprising the less tender parts, will be ground and mixed together with the pork and veal.) Sprinkle them with black pepper and let the rabbit pieces marinate in 1/2 cup cognac overnight. Turn the pieces occasionally to coat them well.

One to two days before you wish to serve the pâté: Grind less tender half of the rabbit meat (not the strips) in the container of a food processor or in a meat grinder. Combine it with the pork, veal, and ground pork fat. Add to this the remaining cognac, the onion, garlic, *épices fines*, salt, pepper, and eggs. Mix the ingredients until thoroughly combined. Taste the mixture for seasoning by frying a small bit in a sauté pan; it should be highly seasoned but not too salty. Adjust the spices accordingly.

Preheat the oven to 350°F.

Line a 2-quart pâté mold with the leaf lard, being sure to overlap the strips slightly as you lay them down. Pack one-third of the pâté mixture into the pan and smooth it down. Decorate it with one-half the marinated rabbit strips, one-half the ham strips, and one-half the hazelnuts. Repeat this procedure and top the strips with the remaining pâté.

Cover the mold and place it in a larger pan. Add hot water to the pan so that it comes halfway up the mold. Bake the terrine for 2 to 2½ hours, or until a sharp knife comes out clean when inserted into the center of the terrine and the juices in the pan are clear yellow. Allow the terrine to cool at room temperature for 30 minutes. Cover the top of the terrine with foil or a plate and place a heavy weight on top of this, for example, a brick or other object. When the terrine has cooled off completely, refrigerate it, with the weight, for at least one day. Remove the weight after one day.

If you plan to keep the terrine a week or two before serving, cover the top of the pâté thoroughly with melted chicken or pork fat to seal it. When you are ready to serve the terrine, dip the bottom of the pan in warm water and unmold the terrine. Serve the terrine at room temperature.

Yield: 12 servings

During the War of 1812, Uncle Sam Wilson, a Troy, New York, meat packer, shipped several hundreds of barrels of pork—each marked with the initials "E.A.U.S."—to our fighting men. Dockworkers unloading these shipments spread the word that they came from "Uncle Sam" (U.S.) who wanted everyone to "eat away" (E.A.). It was in this way that "Uncle Sam," with his generosity and seemingly bottomless pork barrel, came to symbolize not only an American patriarchal figure, but also the United States itself.

◆

Andrew Jackson, in his 1828 campaign for the presidency, called himself a "whole hogger."

◆

North Carolinians, whose state motto was "We Make Pork," commonly led hog drives of some 10,000 to 12,000 animals. There would be a "pig boy" for every hundred head and a manager for every herd. They would seek overnight lodgings in "pig hotels," some of which, like the one built in 1828 by Capt. James Mitchell Alexander in Asheville, N.C., could accommodate some 4,000 hogs and 50 men at a time. It was not unusual during this time for fifteen hotels to exist on one 55-mile stretch of road down south.

◆

In the 1830s American pork consumption was 178 pounds per capita.

◆

The Englishwoman, Mrs. Martineau, traveling in the South in the 1830s, had the following to say: "The dish from which I ate was, according to some, mutton; to others, pork. My own idea is that it was dog."

Reproduced from the collection of the Library of Congress

ONE-POT MEALS

"The Southern consumption of grease—of fat in one form or another—would, I am sure, astonish even an Arctic explorer."

> **—A commentary on the post–Civil War diet by an anonymous, and no doubt Northern, critic**

This section includes perhaps the heartiest and most soul-satisfying recipes of the book. As luncheon or brunch dishes, paired with a salad or simple vegetable accompaniment, these are the perfect dishes for a small family dinner or informal gathering on a crisp autumn or winter day.

Liberties have been taken with the term "one-dish" to have it include not just stews or casseroles, but also savories like pizzas, quiches, and pies that can stand as complete meals on their own.

While most of these recipes are a bit more time-consuming to make than others, they can be prepared ahead of time, even frozen and defrosted, if you wish. In most cases, however, you should allow at least 2 to 3 hours for preparation and cooking time (sometimes longer if the dish requires marinating), plus additional time for reheating if you have made the food in advance. In fact, preparing many of the more highly seasoned dishes a couple of days in advance—for example, the various chilis and tomato-based stews—and allowing the flavors to mellow will enhance their taste enormously.

There are certainly other dishes in the book qualifying for the term "one-dish meals," for example, some of the stir-fried recipes, excluded here because they involve either different cooking methodologies or different cuts of meat. Look for them in the chapter on pages 97–119.

Richard Osborn Cummings wrote in 1840: "A common dish was blood pudding, which was a mixture of hog or sometimes beef blood together with chopped pork seasoned and stuffed in a casing. Hungry laborers would buy a pound of this for three or four cents and make a meal of it with butter crackers. Frequently the laborers raised their own supplies—that is, they notched the ears of scavenger pigs which fed on the offal of the streets. When New York City banished these scavengers by ordinance, the housewives fought with broom and nail the attendants of the hog carts sent about to collect them."

❖

Benjamin Harrison's 1840 campaign song: "He lives in a cabin built of logs,/He plows his own ground and feeds his own hogs."

❖

Dale Brown, in the 1842 book *American Cooking*, wrote: "So much salt pork was eaten by so many Americans in the 19th Century that molasses, the most popular of sweeteners, was regularly used to subdue the briny taste."

❖

In the American South, cotton was king and the pig was queen. By 1860 hogs and other southern livestock numbered half a billion animals, valued at twice as much as the entire cotton crop.

CARNE ADOBADA

Pork is not commonly used in the cuisines of New Mexico and the Southwest, in general. However, the one exception to the rule is carne adobada, *perhaps the best-known pork dish from that region. Serve the stew with flour tortillas, rice, or* posole *for an authentic New Mexican meal.*

24 dried New Mexican chile pods
4 2-inch slices orange peel
2 2-inch slices lemon peel
4 tablespoons orange juice
2 tablespoons cider vinegar
1½ teaspoons salt
1 teaspoon oregano leaves
1 teaspoon ground cumin
¼ teaspoon ground cinnamon
⅛ teaspoon ground cloves
1 lime, juiced
2 garlic cloves, minced
4 tablespoons minced onion
2 tablespoons peanut oil
2 tablespoons tomato paste
2 teaspoons granulated sugar
1½ pounds pork butt or tenderloin, cut into ½ X 3-inch-
long strips
1½ cups water

Rinse off, stem, and seed the dried chile pods, and place them in a bowl with enough hot water to cover them completely. Let the chiles soak for ½ hour, or until they are softened. Remove the chiles from the water. With a butter knife or spoon, scrape out the pulp from each chile, discarding the skin and any tough membranes. You will need approximately 1 cup chile paste.

Combine 1 cup chile paste with the remaining ingredients, except for the pork and the water, in a nonreactive glass or plastic container. Mix them together until you have a smooth paste. Place the pork strips in the chili paste and stir until the pork is well coated. Cover the mixture and let it marinate in the refrigerator overnight.

When ready to cook, place the meat mixture into a casserole and stir in the water. Bring the mixture to a boil. Lower the heat and simmer the stew, uncovered, for 1 hour and 15 minutes to 1½ hours, or until the meat is tender.

Yield: 4 servings

·:·

CHILI VERDE

This is a Tex-Mex–inspired dish in a tomatillo (not to be confused with a green, or unripened red, tomato) sauce. To round out the meal, steam other vegetables like green beans, corn kernels, and zucchini squash together with the potatoes.

½ pound tomatillos
½ lime, juiced
1 garlic clove
1 small onion, cut up
2 fresh jalapeño peppers
6 sprigs fresh coriander (cilantro)
4 sprigs parsley

1 teaspoon sugar
½ teaspoon salt
2 tablespoons peanut oil
1½ pounds boneless pork butt, cut into 1-inch cubes
1 cup water
8 small red potatoes, quartered

Puree the first nine ingredients in the container of a food processor or blender until smooth and well blended.

Heat the oil in a heavy casserole over medium-high heat. Sauté the pork cubes, in batches if necessary to prevent overcrowding, until they are nicely browned on all sides. Add the tomatillo puree and ½ cup of the water to the pork. Bring the mixture to a boil and reduce the heat to a simmer. Cook the chili, uncovered, for 1 hour, stirring occasionally.

Add the potatoes and the remaining ½ cup water to the stew. Cover and simmer the stew another hour, or until the meat and potatoes are tender. If the sauce is too thin, remove the cover and cook the chili a bit longer to let some of the extra liquid evaporate.

Yield: 4 servings

FIRE AND SMOKE CHILI

The debate still rages over what constitutes authentic Texas chili. For purists, the addition of tomatoes, beans, or any other ingredients beside cubed beef and spices is anathema. While this recipe might not be the genuine article in the Lone Star State, it certainly is tasty. Turn up the heat by adding additional hot peppers. (But, remember, the longer the chili cooks, the more the heat in the chilis and cayenne pepper blooms.) If you're planning to make the Chili Lasagna (page 60), use the recipe as is.

6 slices bacon, cut into ¼ X 1-inch-long strips
1 pound boneless pork, cut into 1-inch cubes
1½ pounds beef chuck, cut into 1-inch cubes
1 large red onion, minced
2 small green bell peppers, cubed
3 Anaheim chili peppers, sliced
2 jalapeño peppers, sliced
2 stalks celery, minced
4 garlic cloves, minced
1 ham hock
1 28-ounce can tomatoes in puree
28 ounces (3½ cups) water
1 tablespoon chili powder
1 bay leaf
1 teaspoon ground cumin
1 teaspoon dried oregano
½ teaspoon cayenne pepper (or more, to taste)
1 tablespoon rum
2 tablespoons fine cornmeal (masarepa or masa harina)
Salt and pepper

Cook the bacon pieces in a large casserole or Dutch oven over medium heat until they render their fat and become translucent. Remove the bacon from the pan with a slotted spoon. Add the pork and beef cubes, in batches if necessary to prevent crowding, and cook them over medium-high heat until they are nicely browned all over. Remove the meat with a slotted spoon and set it aside.

Add the onion, fresh peppers, and celery to the pan and sauté them over medium heat until softened. Add the bacon, pork, beef, and all the remaining ingredients except for the cornmeal and salt and pepper. Bring the chili to a boil. Reduce the heat and simmer the stew, uncovered, for approximately 2 hours, or until the meat is tender. Add the cornmeal, and salt and pepper to taste. Simmer an additional 15 minutes, or until the sauce is slightly thickened. Remove the bay leaf before serving.

Yield: 6 to 8 servings

·:·

ITALIAN RAGU

An Italian ragu is more commonly referred to as spaghetti sauce in this country. This version is flavored with ground beef, Italian ham, and Italian bacon. You can also make a more traditional ragu using pieces of boneless pork, veal, and beef. Omit the pancetta, prosciutto, and mushrooms and substitute one-third of a pound of each meat for the ground beef. Brown the meat, and proceed with the recipe in exactly the same way. Before serving, slice the pork, veal, and beef and serve them with the sauce over spaghetti.

2 tablespoons corn oil
1¹/₂-inch-thick piece pancetta (Italian bacon), cut into
   ¹/₄-inch dice

1 large onion, cut into ¼-inch dice
1 stalk celery, cut into ¼-inch dice
2 carrots, cut into ¼-inch dice
12 ounces mushrooms, stemmed and sliced
1 pound ground beef
2 tablespoons vermouth
4 garlic cloves, minced (approximately 1 tablespoon)
1¾ pounds fresh plum tomatoes, peeled, seeded, and halved
1 28-ounce can crushed tomatoes
28 ounces (3½ cups) water
2 tablespoons minced parsley
2 tablespoons tomato paste
2 ounces prosciutto, thinly shredded
¼ cup basil leaves, thinly shredded
1 bay leaf
½ teaspoon black pepper
½ teaspoon dried oregano or 1 teaspoon fresh

Heat the oil in a heavy casserole or saucepan over medium-high heat. Add the pancetta to the pan and sauté it, stirring frequently, until it is golden in color. Add the onion, celery, and carrots to the pancetta, and continue cooking the mixture over medium heat until the vegetables are softened, about 5 to 7 minutes. Add the mushrooms to the vegetables, and cook them until they are softened. Finally, add the beef to the vegetables, and cook it over medium-high heat until almost completely cooked through and just slightly pink. Add the vermouth to the sauce over high heat, and boil the mixture for 2 minutes.

Reduce the heat to low and add all of the remaining ingredients. Cook the ragu at a bare simmer for several hours (the longer the better) until it is very thick and all the excess water has evaporated. At a minimum, cook the sauce 3 to 4 hours. Cooking for 5 to 6 hours would improve the flavor immensely. Remove the bay leaf before serving.

Yield: 4 generous servings

PANAMA RED STEW

Back during gold rush days, '49'ers en route to California often boarded ships that traveled from New York or Florida to California via Panama, Cuba, Jamaica, Chile, Trinidad, or Tobago. The following recipe, kind of a cross between a pork bourguignon and a chili, is based upon a '49'ers account of foods he encountered in Panama on his way to gold territory. Not surprisingly, this type of dish was mentioned as being popular in almost all the states along the shipping route as well, including New York, Florida, and California.

3 ounces bacon, cut into ¼ X 1-inch strips
1½ pounds pork shoulder or sirloin, cut into 1½-inch cubes
¼ cup flour seasoned with salt and pepper
1 large onion, chopped (1½ cups)
½ large green pepper, cut into small cubes (½ cup)
1 large celery stalk, chopped (½ cup)
1 tablespoon vegetable oil
1 cup red Bordeaux wine
½ 28-ounce can of Italian plum tomatoes with their juice
2 garlic cloves, minced
1 bay leaf
1 heaping tablespoon tomato paste
¼ teaspoon dried oregano
½ cup pitted, quartered black olives, such as Kalamata
Ground red pepper to taste
½ pound mushrooms, quartered, sautéed in 2 tablespoons
**   butter**
Salt and black pepper

Sauté the bacon strips in a heavy casserole over medium heat until they are cooked through but not browned. Remove the bacon with a slotted spoon.

Dredge the pork cubes in the seasoned flour. Shake off the excess flour, and sauté the pork cubes in the hot bacon fat until they are nicely browned. Remove the meat and set it aside. Add the onion, green pepper, and celery to the pan, along with the oil (if necessary). Sauté the vegetables until they become soft and golden yellow, and scrape up any browned bits on the bottom of the pan.

Add all the remaining ingredients, except for the mushrooms and salt and pepper. Bring the stew to a boil and lower the heat to a simmer. Cook the stew, covered, for approximately 2 hours, or until the meat is tender. Skim the fat from the stew and add the sautéed mushrooms. Season with salt and black pepper to taste. Remove the bay leaf before serving.

Yield: 4 servings

·:·

PHILIPPINE ADOBO

Years before the infamous Ferdinand and Imelda Marcos sought asylum in the United States, Filipinos were (and remain) one of the largest immigrant groups in our country. As part of Douglas MacArthur's forces, Filipinos fought side by side with American soldiers against the Japanese during World War II. In grateful acknowledgment for their service, Filipinos were permitted to emigrate to the United States to become naturalized citizens. Ingredients used in Philippine adobado or adobo (meaning "pickled meat") are different from other Spanish-style preparations of the same name, but produce an equally delicious end result. Serve over Chinese-style noodles or rice.

2 garlic cloves, minced
⅔ cup soy sauce
¼ cup white vinegar
½ teaspoon black pepper
1 tablespoon tamarind paste (available in Asian markets)
1 pound pork, cut into ½-inch cubes
4 tablespoons peanut oil
1 large onion, thinly sliced
1 pound Chinese cabbage, thinly sliced

Combine the first five ingredients in a nonreactive bowl or container. Add the pork cubes and let them marinate for several hours or overnight in the refrigerator. Bring the meat to room temperature ½ hour before cooking.

Drain the meat and reserve the marinade. Pat the meat dry.

Heat the peanut oil in a wok or deep sauté pan over high heat. Add the meat cubes to the hot oil and stir-fry them until they are cooked through and nicely browned, approximately 5 to 7 minutes. Remove the meat with a slotted spoon and set it aside.

Add the onion to the pan and stir-fry it until it is soft and wilted. Add the cabbage and the reserved marinade, and cook the cabbage until it is wilted and the liquid is slightly reduced. Add the pork cubes and toss the stir-fry until it is combined and heated through. Serve immediately.

Yield: 4 servings

PORK AU VINAIGRE

This recipe is adapted from one that originally called for lamb as the main ingredient. It works well with pork, too, and is surprisingly delicate tasting, despite the amount of vinegar.

2 tablespoons olive oil
1 large onion, chopped
1½ pounds boneless pork butt, cut into 1-inch cubes
½ cup good-quality champagne vinegar
¼ cup raspberry vinegar
½ cup water
Salt and pepper
¾ pound trimmed green beans

Heat the oil in a large casserole over a medium flame. Add the onion to the pan and sauté it until it is translucent. Add the pork cubes, in batches if necessary to prevent crowding, and sauté them until they are browned on all sides.

Add the vinegars and water to the casserole. Sprinkle the meat with salt and pepper. Add the green beans in a layer on top and sprinkle them with salt and pepper. Bring the stew to a boil and lower the heat to a simmer.

Cook the stew, covered, for approximately 1½ hours, or until the meat is tender.

Yield: 4 servings

PORK STEW WITH DRIED FRUITS

Before refrigeration became available, most fresh foods, including meats and fruits, were preserved by salting or drying to last through the winter months. A stew of dried fruits (especially apples) and pork was an American staple dating back to colonial times. This version uses prunes, apricots, and figs. But any other combination of dried fruits would work equally well.

6 ounces each *pitted sour prunes, dried apricots, and dried*
   figs, quartered
1 cup strong brewed tea
2 tablespoons vegetable oil
1½ pounds pork butt or shoulder, cut into 1-inch cubes
⅓ cup flour, seasoned with salt and pepper to taste
1 large onion, minced
1 cup dry white wine
3 tablespoons Grand Marnier or other orange-flavored
   brandy
3 cloves
½ cinnamon stick
½ teaspoon dried thyme
1 3-inch strip orange peel
Salt and pepper

Soak the prunes, apricots, and figs in the tea until they are softened, about ½ hour. Drain the fruit, but reserve the soaking liquid.

Heat the oil in a Dutch oven or other large heavy pan over a medium-high flame. Dredge the pork cubes in the seasoned flour and sauté them in the hot oil, in batches if necessary to prevent crowding, until browned. Remove the pork cubes with a slotted spoon and set them aside. Sauté the onion in the pan, scraping up the browned bits, until golden, approximately 5 to 7 minutes.

Add the pork cubes, dried fruits, white wine, liqueur, spices, thyme, orange peel, and ¼ cup reserved soaking liquid to the pan. Bring the mixture to a boil for 1 minute. Lower the heat and simmer, covered, for 1½ to 2 hours, or until the pork is cooked through and soft. Add salt and pepper to taste.

Yield: 4 servings

·:·

CHICKEN AND SAUSAGE HASH

This breakfast or brunch dish is a perfect way to use up leftover chicken. If you prefer to make the chicken fresh, just poach one or two chicken breasts in water or flavored broth for 20 to 30 minutes, or until they are cooked through.

1 pound white potatoes, peeled and cut into ½-inch cubes
1 large carrot, cut into ½-inch cubes
½ pound sage-flavored breakfast sausage
1 small onion, minced
¾ teaspoon minced garlic
⅓ cup frozen peas
6 ounces cooked chicken, cut into ½-inch cubes
1 tablespoon vegetable oil
Salt and pepper

Preheat the oven to 350°F.

Place the potatoes in a small saucepan with enough salted water to barely cover them. Bring the water to a simmer and cook the potatoes until they are soft, approximately 5 minutes. Drain the potatoes and place them in a medium mixing bowl. Cook the carrots in the same manner, and add them to the bowl with the potatoes.

Sauté the sausage in a skillet over medium heat until it is cooked through. Remove the sausage with a slotted spoon and add it to the potatoes and carrots. Sauté the onion and garlic in the skillet over medium heat until softened and golden-colored, approximately 5 to 7 minutes. Remove the onion with a slotted spoon and add it to the sausage along with the peas, chicken, and oil. Season with salt and pepper to taste.

Place the hash into an 8-inch round pan, packing it down firmly with the back of a spoon. Bake it for 15 minutes, or until it is heated through. Run the hash under the broiler for 1 to 2 minutes to brown it on top. Cut the hash into portions and serve immediately.

Yield: 4 servings

∴

CHILI LASAGNA

Italian lasagna goes Western! This is a really delicious dish, perfect for informal parties. The traditional béchamel sauce is replaced by a white bean and sour cream puree, and that boring tomato sauce is spiced up and chunky.

1 19-ounce can white kidney beans, drained
4 green onions, thinly sliced
½ cup sour cream
1 teaspoon salt
1 recipe Fire and Smoke Chili (page 51)
1 pound lasagna noodles, cooked according to package
    directions
4 ounces shredded Monterey Jack cheese (approximately 2
    cups)
4 ounces shredded sharp cheddar cheese (approximately 2
    cups)

Preheat the oven to 350°F.

Place the kidney beans in a small bowl and mash them with a potato masher. Add the green onions, sour cream, and salt to the beans and mix until smooth and thoroughly combined.

Ladle a bit of sauce from the chili over the bottom of a lasagna pan or a 9 X 13-inch oblong pan. Lay one-third of the lasagna noodles over the sauce. Next, spoon about a third of the chili over the noodles. On top of the chili, spread half of the bean mixture. Sprinkle the bean paste with a third of the shredded Jack and cheddar cheeses. Repeat this procedure again. Top the lasagna with the remaining third of the noodles and enough sauce from the chili to cover the noodles evenly (try not to add too many meat chunks to the top layer). Sprinkle the top of the lasagna with the remaining cheese.

Bake the lasagna for ½ hour, or until it is bubbling and the cheese is melted and browned on top. For a neater presentation, allow the lasagna to cool at room temperature for 10 minutes before serving.

Yield: 8 to 10 generous servings

CORNISH PASTIES

Tin miners from Cornwall, England, where the remains of ancient tin mines still exist, emigrated to the midwestern states of Wisconsin, Michigan, and Minnesota in the 1830s. One of the native dishes they brought with them was Cornish Pasties, envelopes of dough in the shape of a miner's lunch pail. They were a one-handed, portable whole meal in a package, comprised of meat at one end, vegetables in the middle, and fruit at the other end. The miners' wives would bake and wrap the pies in the morning so that they would still be warm for lunch. Pasty making became something of an art; the shape of the pie itself and even the design on top would indicate what was inside. The pies are something of a novelty, and might be fun to make for a picnic or tailgate party.

2 pounds puff pastry

MEAT FILLING

1 tablespoon vegetable oil
1 small onion, minced
½ pound ground pork
2 tablespoons white wine
1 garlic clove, minced
1½ tablespoons minced parsley
Salt and pepper

VEGETABLE FILLING

1 tablespoon butter
¾ pound savoy cabbage, cored and shredded
2 leeks, cleaned and shredded
2 large carrots, grated
Salt and pepper

FRUIT FILLING

2 medium tart apples, such as Granny Smith or New
    Zealand Braeburn
1½ teaspoons lemon juice
3 tablespoons sugar
¼ teaspoon cinnamon
⅛ teaspoon nutmeg
1 tablespoon flour

1 egg, beaten with 1 tablespoon water

Divide the puff pastry into quarters. Roll each quarter into a rectangle ¼-inch thick, measuring 10 X 16 inches. Place the pastry on a baking sheet and chill it in the refrigerator for 1 hour.

Make the meat filling: Heat the vegetable oil in a frying pan over medium heat. Add the onion and sauté it until it becomes translucent and golden, approximately 5 minutes. Add the ground pork to the onion and sauté it. When almost completely cooked through, add the wine and the garlic. Turn the heat to high and boil the mixture for 2 minutes. Remove the pan from the heat and add the parsley, salt, and pepper. Let the meat filling cool to room temperature.

Make the vegetable filling: Melt the butter in a Dutch oven or large sauté pan over low heat. Add the cabbage, leeks, and carrots and cook, covered, for ½ hour. Season with salt and pepper to taste.

Make the fruit filling: Peel and slice the apples. Cut the slices into small chunks and toss them with the lemon juice. Mix in all the remaining ingredients.

To assemble the pies: Take approximately ⅓ cup of each filling and place them, meat, vegetable, fruit, lengthwise along the center third of the pastry, leaving a ½-inch border at the edges. Moisten the edges with water. Fold in the two sides of the pastry to enclose the filling (into a rectangle measuring 10 X 8 inches), pressing down lightly along the edges. Using the dull side of a knife, make indentations along the edge of the pastry at ½-inch intervals, to create a scalloped border. With the tip of the knife, press down to make a small V-shaped indentation in each of the scallops to further seal the pastry. Brush the pastry with the egg wash, being careful not to let it drip down the edges of the pastry, and chill the pies in the refrigerator for 1 hour. Repeat with the remaining filling and pastry.

Preheat the oven to 375°F.

Remove the pasties from the refrigerator and brush them with the egg wash again. Bake them for 35 minutes, or until nicely puffed and golden brown.

Yield: 4 servings (4 pasties)

·:·

PORK AND DUCK SAUSAGE PIZZA

Although this recipe makes wonderful use of Pork and Duck Sausages (page 92), store-bought duck or other sausages can be substituted, if desired. Different types of cheese can be used as well to add interest.

1 pound Pork and Duck Sausages (page 92)
1 large red bell pepper
1 pound store-bought or homemade pizza dough, ready to use
1 cup tomato sauce, preferably homemade
2 teaspoons minced garlic
1 tablespoon chopped fresh basil, if available

¹/₄ pound mozzarella cheese, grated
¹/₄ pound Bel Paese cheese, grated
¹/₄ pound Gruyère cheese, grated
2 tablespoons olive oil

Preheat the oven to 500°F. for 30 minutes.

Prick the sausages all over with a fork, and place them in a saucepan with water to cover them over medium heat. Bring the water to a boil. Lower the heat and simmer the sausages until they are cooked through and no longer pink, approximately 10 minutes. Drain the sausages. When cool enough to handle, slice the sausages into ¼-inch rounds.

Char the bell pepper over an open flame until it is completely blackened and blistered. Place the pepper in a small paper bag and seal it. After 5 minutes, remove the pepper and peel it. Slice the pepper into thin strips.

Stretch and roll out the pizza dough to fit a 15-inch pizza pan. Press the dough into the pan and build up a thickened rim for the crust. Spread the tomato sauce onto the dough and top it with the sausage slices. Sprinkle with the garlic and basil. Arrange the bell pepper strips artistically atop the pizza, and top it off with the cheeses. Sprinkle the pizza with the olive oil.

Bake the pizza for 15 to 20 minutes, or until it is golden and bubbly.

Yield: 4 servings (6 to 8 slices)

EMPANADAS

These flaky, savory pastries are of Hispanic origin. They are nice to have as a hot hors d'oeuvre or a light lunch.

1 large sweet potato (approximately ⅓ pound), peeled and cut into ¼-inch cubes
2 tablespoons vegetable oil
1 medium onion, minced
1 pound ground pork
¼ cup white wine
2 garlic cloves, minced
½ cup pitted green olives, quartered
¼ cup raisins
¼ teaspoon cinnamon
½ teaspoon hot paprika
Salt and pepper
Empanada Dough (page 67)
Vegetable oil for cooking

Place the sweet potato cubes in a small saucepan with enough salted water to barely cover them. Bring the water to a boil and simmer the potatoes until they are tender, about 5 minutes. Drain, cool, and set aside the cooked sweet potatoes.

Heat the oil in a sauté pan over medium heat. Add the onion and cook it until it becomes golden and translucent, approximately 5 minutes. Add the pork to the sauté pan and cook it until the meat is just slightly pink. Turn the heat to high, add the wine and garlic, and boil the meat mixture over high heat for 2 minutes. Remove the pan from the heat. Add the sweet potato and remaining ingredients (except Empanada Dough and vegetable oil) to the pork. Season the mixture with salt and pepper to taste. Let the filling cool to room temperature.

Roll out the Empanada Dough into a 12-inch rope and cut it into 1-inch pieces. Form each piece into a small ball. Roll each ball into a 6-inch circle. Keep the circles covered as you work.

Place ¼ cup filling on each circle. Moisten the edges of the dough with water. Fold over and seal the dough into a half-moon shape, enclosing the filling completely. Repeat with the remaining dough and filling.

To cook the empanadas, pour the vegetable oil into a deep heavy sauté pan or fryer to a depth of three inches. Heat the oil to 375°F. Add the empanadas in batches to the hot oil and cook the empanadas, turning them occasionally, until golden brown, about 2 minutes. Drain the empanadas on paper towels and serve them immediately.

Yield: 4 to 6 servings (12 empanadas)

EMPANADA DOUGH

¼ teaspoon turmeric
5 to 6 tablespoons ice water
1½ cups flour
1 teaspoon salt
⅓ cup solid vegetable shortening

Dissolve the turmeric in the ice water.

Combine the flour and salt in the container of a food processor. Using on-off pulses, cut in the shortening until it forms particles the size of peas. With the motor running, add the ice water a tablespoon at a time, until the dough forms a ball. Remove the dough from the processor bowl and knead it on a lightly floured surface 30 seconds, or until it is smooth.

Follow the directions for shaping the dough in the empanada recipe.

SOUTHWESTERN QUICHE

A hearty southwestern breakfast might include chorizo and scrambled eggs wrapped in a flour torilla and topped with cheese and chili sauce. Here we have a slightly more refined version of this taste combination, designed for real men—and women—who still eat quiche.

**1 9-inch piecrust, either store-bought or homemade
    (page 69)**
¼ pound Chorizo Sausage (page 79)
1 small onion, minced
1¾ cups heavy cream
4 eggs
1 tablespoon tomato paste
2 ounces cheddar cheese, shredded (approximately 1 cup)
**2 ounces Monterey Jack cheese, shredded (approximately 1
    cup)**
Salt, freshly grated nutmeg, and cayenne pepper to taste
**3 pickled jalapeño peppers, stemmed, seeded, and sliced into
    thin rounds**

Partially bake the piecrust according to the manufacturer's instructions or following the instructions on page 69. Turn the oven temperature to 375°F.

While preparing the crust, sauté the chorizo in a small pan until it is browned and cooked through. Remove the sausage with a slotted spoon and set it aside to cool. Add the onion to the sauté pan and cook it until it becomes golden and translucent. Add the onion to the sausage.

In a large measuring cup, beat lightly with a fork the cream, eggs, and tomato paste until they are well combined. Stir in the cheeses and seasonings to taste.

Scatter the onion and sausage mixture over the bottom of the partially baked piecrust. Cover the sausage with the egg mixture. Decorate the top of the pie with the jalapeño slices and bake the quiche for 30 minutes, or until the egg custard is set and nicely browned on top.

Yield: 4 to 6 servings

.:.

PIECRUST

1 1/2 cups flour
1 teaspoon salt
1 1/2 sticks butter, cut into small pieces
4 to 5 tablespoons cold water
1 egg yolk, beaten with 1 tablespoon water

Combine the flour, salt, and butter in the container of a food processor. Pulse the mixture until the butter has formed pea-sized particles. With the motor running, gradually add the water, just enough so that the dough pulls together and forms a ball.

Wrap the dough in plastic wrap, flatten it into a disk shape, and chill it in the refrigerator at least 30 minutes.

On a floured surface, roll out the dough to fit a 9-inch quiche or pie plate. Prick the bottom of the shell lightly with a fork and chill it in the refrigerator for at least 15 minutes. Preheat the oven to 400 °F.

Line the piecrust with aluminum foil or parchment paper and fill it with beans or pie weights. Bake the shell in the preheated oven for 10 minutes. Remove the beans and foil and continue to bake the shell for 3 minutes more. Remove the shell from the oven and brush the bottom and sides of the crust with the egg yolk wash to seal it.

Yield: 1 9-inch piecrust

George Frederick describes culinary life in the early twentieth century in a Pennsylvania Dutch family: "With meat grinders, large mixing bowls and sausage stuffing machines, my grandparents would produce, before my astounded young eyes, a wide variety of foods, fresh pork sausage, smoked beef and beef sausage, Lebanon style bologna, highly spiced . . . the bologna, five inches in diameter, is probably over-spiced for most tastes, but it is surely appetizing."

◆

"Sausage making was a gala night with the family. The scraps which came from trimming the hams, shoulders, and other pieces were made into sausages, for which purpose they must be thoroughly 'chopped.' We had no meat cutters such as the stores furnish now, but we had a chopping bench, a plank six or eight feet long set up on four legs, and narrow pieces nailed on all the sides so as to make a shallow box, into which the meat was put. With axes and hatchets the younger members of the family had the chopping to do. By the time we thought it was fine enough, the choppers were usually tired. My grandmother used to caution us not to chop it too fine or it would be poisonous; but when we became tired as we always did, and would ask if we might quit, she would say no. We at last concluded that she only meant we could not chop it too fine." A recollection of nineteenth-century Virginia farm life from John Jay Janney.

◆

President Warren G. Harding, whenever he invited his card-playing friends over for a round of poker, had a standing order with the White House chef: Knockwurst and sauerkraut.

THE POLICE, UNDER THE DIRECTION OF INSPECTOR DOWNING, CLEARING THE PIGGERIES OF BERNARD KELLY

***Engraving by H.L.S. in Frank Leslie's
Illustrated Newspaper, August 13, 1859.***

*Courtesy of the New York Historical Society,
New York City*

SAUSAGES
AND GROUND
PORK

Annual U.S. sausage production in the 1940s was 700 million links, which "if placed in links sixteen to the pound would reach from the earth to the moon and back and leave enough to wrap the earth at the equator eight times."

—ANONYMOUS

Undeniably sausages remain an American favorite. One advertising executive was onto something when he proclaimed hot dogs (along with baseball, apple pie, and Chevrolet automobiles) as quintessentially American. However, Americans are not unique in their love of links. In fact, there are probably hundreds of sausage varieties produced by different regions or ethnic groups both here and abroad.

Sausages are a venerable culinary preparation eaten in ancient times by Greeks, Romans, and, no doubt, countless other civilizations. A favorite food associated with community events, harvest festivals, feast days, and rituals involving animal sacrifices, sausages were often made by stuffing an animal's stomach or intestines with a mixture of chopped seasoned meat, fat, blood, and grain and roasting them over a fire—a method of preparation that has changed little over the ages.

Of the wide variety of smoked, fresh, or dried sausages available commercially from corner delis, gourmet shops, and companies specializing in sausage making, some are more familiar— hot dogs, bologna, salami, knockwurst, breakfast sausages, for example—while others—chorizo, kielbasa, linguiça, andouille, merguez, boudin blanc—are a bit more exotic sounding and tasting. Contemporary chefs and sausage makers have promoted something of a sausage renaissance and have shown great creativity in devising new and unusual types of sausages made from seafood, game, beans, vegetables, and almost every ingredient imaginable. And that is one of the beauties of sausages: versatility, limited only by the cook's imagination.

When there are so many wonderful sausage products available, you may wonder, is it worthwhile to make them at home? Homemade sausages are far fresher and better tasting than the average store-bought variety, and they are fun to make. You can control the amount of salt and fat that goes into your own sausages and adjust their flavoring to your taste.

Not much special equipment is needed to prepare sausages. A meat grinder equipped with a sausage stuffing horn or a food processor and manual stuffer make quick work of the process. Or, if you do not own this type of equipment, a pastry bag outfitted with a one-inch plain tip can be a makeshift sausage stuffer. (Be forewarned that the pastry bag method requires a lot of elbow grease, or, better yet, a muscular cooking partner.) But you can forego the grinding and stuffing process altogether if you wish. Just have your butcher grind together the meat(s) and fat for you, season the mixture yourself, form it into patties or meatballs, and cook.

Sausage meat formed into logs can also be poached in plastic wrap. Lay the meat mixture in the center of a large double thickness of plastic wrap to form a sausagelike shape. Fold over one edge of the plastic wrap to cover the meat and continue to roll the sausage until thoroughly enclosed. Twist one end of the package very tightly and knot it twice. Repeat the twisting and knotting with the other side. Poach the sausage roll in simmering water until cooked through.

Whatever method you choose for making your sausages, there are a few things you should keep in mind:

♦ All sausages do need a certain percentage of fat to keep them moist and tasty. While animal fat in its various forms may be anathema in today's cholesterol-obsessed world, it is a necessary evil in sausage making. A proportion of 2½ to 3 parts lean meat to 1 part fat is a general rule of thumb. The sausage recipes that follow tend toward the leaner side.

♦ Salt, the evil stepsister of cholesterol, is also required when preparing sausages. A rough guideline is approximately 1 tablespoon coarse kosher salt per 2 pounds meat/fat mixture. Of course, you can add more if you wish.

♦ Tasting and adjusting the sausage mixture for salt and seasonings is essential. To do this, fry a small quantity of the sausage in a sauté pan until cooked through. Taste the sausage and add additional herbs and spices as you wish. Then sample it again. Remember, however, it is always easier to add more than to take away.

The following section contains sausage recipes, both traditional and unusual, and recipes using sausages in combination with other ingredients. Ground pork recipes have been included here as well.

Frederic Klees, a Pennsylvania historian, wrote: "One wonders how the Philadelphians got along for a whole year—that of 1682—until the Pennsylvania Dutch arrived and gave them scrapple."

During a visit to North America in the 1800s nineteen-year-old Prince Edward VII of Wales, not known for his intelligence, was believed to have sampled this delicacy in Philadelphia. He remarked: "I met a large and interesting family named Scrapple, and I discovered a rather delicious native food they call biddle." Reportedly the Biddle family took the comment in good-natured stride.

BRATWURST

For some reason, Sheboygan, Wisconsin, is the bratwurst capital of the world. Who knows why Sheboyganites cannot get enough of this German-style white sausage? Here is a light version, which uses a combination of chicken and pork. Braised Red Cabbage (page 167) would be a perfect accompaniment.

2 lengths sausage casing
1 pound boneless chicken breasts, skinned
2 ounces onion
1 pound pork butt or shoulder, cut up
¾ pound pork fat

1 cup fresh bread crumbs (approximately 4 slices of bread)
½ cup milk
1 tablespoon kosher salt
½ teaspoon nutmeg
¼ teaspoon mace
1 teaspoon white pepper

Prepare the sausage casings by first rinsing them off in cold water. Let them soak in cold water for a few minutes. Then take each casing and attach its opening to a water faucet. Turn on the tap and flush the casing with water. (If there are any holes in the casing, discard it.) Let the casings soak in fresh cool water until they are needed.

Grind the chicken, onion, pork, and pork fat through the fine blade of a meat grinder. Or process the meat in batches in the container of a food processor, using on-off pulses to start. Process the mixture until it is somewhat smooth in consistency. Add the remaining ingredients to the meat, and mix them together until they are thoroughly combined and slightly sticky.

Fry a small amount of the meat mixture in a sauté pan over medium-high heat until it is cooked through. Taste the sausage for seasoning and adjust it accordingly. Refrigerate the sausage mixture for 1 hour.

Wring out the excess water from the sausage casings. Attach one end of the sausage casing to a sausage stuffing horn or other similar device. Push the length of the casing up onto the horn but leave several inches overhanging at the end. Knot the free end and proceed to stuff the casing loosely with the sausage mixture. Form the sausages into 4-inch lengths. To do this, pinch the stuffed casing at 4-inch intervals and twist several times in opposite directions to secure each link.

Yield: 16 sausages (4 to 6 servings)

BREAKFAST SAUSAGES

Recipes for sage-flavored breakfast sausage, in patties or links, date back to the earliest of American cookbooks. You can add more sage powder, or less, according to taste. Try the sausages plain for breakfast or in the Chicken and Sausage Hash (page 59).

1 to 2 lengths sausage casing
1 pound boneless pork butt or shoulder, cut into cubes
½ pound pork fat
1 tablespoon kosher salt
2 teaspoons powdered sage (more or less, to taste)
¾ teaspoon black pepper

Prepare the sausage casings by first rinsing them off in cold water. Let them soak in cold water for a few minutes. Then take each casing and attach its opening to a water faucet. Turn on the tap and flush the casing with water. (If there are any holes in the casing, discard it.) Let the casings soak in fresh cool water until they are needed.

Grind the pork and pork fat through the fine blade of a meat grinder. Or process the meat in batches in the container of a food processor, using on-off pulses to start. Process the mixture until it is somewhat smooth in consistency. Add the remaining ingredients to the meat, and mix them together until they are thoroughly combined and slightly sticky.

Fry a small amount of the meat mixture in a sauté pan over medium-high heat until it is cooked through. Taste the sausage for seasoning and adjust it accordingly. Refrigerate the sausage mixture for 1 hour.

Wring out the excess water from the sausage casings. Attach one end of the sausage casing to a sausage stuffing horn or other similar device. Push the length of the casing up onto the horn but leave several inches overhanging at the end. Knot the free end and proceed to stuff the casing loosely with the sausage mixture. Form the sausages into 3-inch lengths. To do this, pinch the stuffed casing at 3-inch intervals and twist several times in opposite directions to secure each link.

Yield: 12 sausages (6 servings)

·:·

CHORIZO SAUSAGE

Chorizo is a Spanish-style sausage, spicy with red pepper. This version is based on one tasted in New Mexico. It is a little bit different because it uses whole coriander and cumin seed to add extra flavor to the meat. As always, you can adjust the amount of spice and heat to your own taste. Use the chorizo in the Southwestern Quiche (page 68). It would also be equally as tasty in a paella or other rice dish.

1 length sausage casing
1 pound boneless pork butt or shoulder, cut into cubes
1/3 pound pork fat
1 tablespoon kosher salt
2 garlic cloves, minced
1 1/2 teaspoons red pepper flakes
1 teaspoon coriander seed, lightly crushed
1 1/2 teaspoons cumin seed, lightly crushed
1/2 teaspoon black pepper

Prepare the sausage casing by first rinsing it off in cold water. Let it soak in cold water for a few minutes. Then take the casing and attach its opening to a water faucet. Turn on the tap and flush the casing with water. (If there are any holes in the casing, discard it.) Let the casing soak in fresh cool water until it is needed.

Grind the pork and pork fat through the fine blade of a meat grinder. Or process the meat in batches in the container of a food processor, using on-off pulses to start. Process the mixture until it is somewhat smooth in consistency. Add the remaining ingredients to the meat, and mix them together until they are thoroughly combined and slightly sticky.

Fry a small amount of the meat mixture in a sauté pan over medium-high heat until it is cooked through. Taste the sausage for seasoning and adjust it accordingly. Refrigerate the sausage mixture for 1 hour.

Wring out the excess water from the sausage casings. Attach one end of the sausage casing to a sausage stuffing horn or other similar device. Push the length of the casing up onto the horn but leave several inches overhanging at the end. Knot the free end and proceed to stuff the casing loosely with the sausage mixture. Form the sausages into 3-inch lengths. To do this, pinch the stuffed casing at 3-inch intervals and twist several times in opposite directions to secure each link.

Yield: 12 sausages (4 servings)

HOT DOGS

What could be more American than the hot dog? It was invented in St. Louis, Missouri, in 1883 by a gentleman named Anton Ludwig Feuchtwanger, who called it a frankfurter. Served in a split bun, it became an overnight sensation. The sobriquet "hot dog" was coined in 1890 by a cartoonist, "Tad" Dorgan.

2 lengths sausage casing
1 pound beef chuck, cut into cubes
1 pound pork butt or shoulder, cut into cubes
¾ pound pork fat
2 ounces onion
1½ tablespoons kosher salt
1½ tablespoons minced garlic
1 teaspoon paprika

Prepare the sausage casings by first rinsing them off in cold water. Let them soak in cold water for a few minutes. Then take each casing and attach its opening to a water faucet. Turn on the tap and flush the casing with water. (If there are any holes in the casing, discard it.) Let the casings soak in fresh cool water until they are needed.

Grind the beef, pork, pork fat, and onion through the fine blade of a meat grinder *twice*. Or process the meat in batches in the container of a food processor, using on-off pulses to start. Process the mixture until it is fairly smooth in consistency. (Hot dogs should have a smoother texture than regular sausages.) Add the remaining ingredients to the meat, and mix them together until they are thoroughly combined and slightly sticky.

Fry a small amount of the meat mixture in a sauté pan over medium-high heat until it is cooked through. Taste the sausage for seasoning and adjust it accordingly. Refrigerate the sausage mixture for 1 hour.

Wring out the excess water from the sausage casings. Attach one end of the sausage casing to a sausage stuffing horn or other similar device. Push the length of the casing up onto the horn but leave several inches overhanging at the end. Knot the free end and proceed to stuff the casing loosely with the sausage mixture. Form the sausages into 6-inch lengths. To do this, pinch the stuffed casing at 6-inch intervals and twist several times in opposite directions to secure each link.

Yield: 12 sausages (6 servings)

INDIAN PORK BURGERS

The vast majority of Indians from subcontinental Asia are not pork eaters. In fact, a rebellion broke out in India in 1857 when Muslim troops refused to unpack British ammunition packed in lard. Despite religious and ethical prohibitions against touching, let alone eating, the pig, pork does marry well with Indian curry, as you will see with this version of that old American standby, the hamburger.

½ **pound ground pork**
½ **pound ground turkey**
¼ **cup minced onion**
¼ **cup mango chutney**
2 small garlic cloves, minced
2 tablespoons chopped fresh coriander (cilantro)
1 teaspoon curry powder
1 teaspoon salt
4 hamburger buns or rolls
Sliced sweet onion
Sliced cucumber
Sliced tomato
Mango chutney

Combine the first eight ingredients in a bowl, and mix them lightly with a fork until they are just combined. Divide the meat into 4 equal portions and form each into a large flat patty, about ½-inch thick.

Cook the patties under a preheated broiler or on a charcoal fire approximately 5 to 6 minutes per side, or until cooked completely through. Serve on the buns with the sliced vegetables and chutney as garnishes.

Yield: 4 servings

ITALIAN SAUSAGE

Fennel-flavored "Italian" sausage is certainly one of America's best-loved and familiar favorites. But did you know that an Italian pignoli-flavored sausage was so favored and figured so prominently in the pagan feasts and public debauchery of ancient Rome that it was deemed sinful and banned by Constantine the Great, subsequent emperors, and the Christian Church following the fall of Rome? This created a brisk trade in bootlegged sausage. Herewith a contemporary version of the sinful sausage.

2 lengths sausage casing
1 pound boneless veal, cut into cubes
1 pound boneless pork shoulder or butt, cut into cubes
⅔ pound pork fat
2 tablespoons kosher salt
6 tablespoons toasted pine nuts, coarsely chopped
1 tablespoon dried rosemary, crumbled
1 tablespoon fennel seeds, crushed
1 teaspoon black pepper

Prepare the sausage casings by first rinsing them off in cold water. Let them soak in cold water for a few minutes. Then take each casing and attach its opening to a water faucet. Turn on the tap and flush the casing with water. (If there are any holes in the casing, discard it.) Let the casings soak in fresh cool water until they are needed.

Grind the veal, pork, and pork fat through the fine blade of a meat grinder. Or process the meat in batches in the container of a food processor, using on-off pulses to start. Process the mixture until it is somewhat smooth in consistency. Add the remaining ingredients to the meat, and mix them together until they are thoroughly combined and slightly sticky.

Fry a small amount of the meat mixture in a sauté pan over medium-high heat until it is cooked through. Taste the sausage for seasoning and adjust it accordingly. Refrigerate the sausage mixture for 1 hour.

Wring out the excess water from the sausage casings. Attach one end of the sausage casing to a sausage stuffing horn or other similar device. Push the length of the casing up onto the horn but leave several inches overhanging at the end. Knot the free end and proceed to stuff the casing loosely with the sausage mixture. Form the sausages into 4-inch lengths. To do this, pinch the stuffed casing at 4-inch intervals and twist several times in opposite directions to secure each link.

Yield: 16 sausages (4 to 6 servings)

ITALIAN SAUSAGES WITH PIPERADE

The Italian sausage, grilled with peppers and onions, is quintessential New York City street food, served everywhere from the San Gennaro Festival in Little Italy, to the Ninth Avenue Food Fair on the West Side, to the food carts along Museum Mile on the East Side. Here is a recipe that would please New Yorkers and non–New Yorkers alike.

2 tablespoons vegetable oil
1 large onion, thinly sliced
1 each large green, red, and yellow bell pepper, cored and
      thinly sliced
1 ½ teaspoons chopped garlic
½ teaspoon black pepper
1 teaspoon salt
1 ½ teaspoons balsamic vinegar
8 Italian sausages

Heat the oil in a large sauté pan or skillet over medium heat. Add the onions and peppers and cook them until they are softened, approximately 10 minutes. Lower the heat and add the remaining ingredients (except for the sausages) and cook the mixture, uncovered, stirring occasionally, until the peppers and onions are very soft and lightly brown, approximately 20 to 30 minutes. Taste and adjust for seasonings.

Preheat the broiler or prepare a charcoal or electric grill. Cook the sausages approximately 5 minutes per side, or until they are cooked through and no longer pink inside. Serve the sausages with the pepper and onion mixture.

Yield: 4 servings

K. C.'s MEAT LOAF "AMERICAINE"

The French "Sauce Americaine" is a tomato-based one, which, some have suggested, refers derogatorily to the American habit of dousing everything with ketchup. We thumbed our noses at the French back in the French and Indian Wars and we can do it again. Here is a meat loaf recipe calling for ketchup as an ingredient. Of course, to truly savor it, serve it with ketchup on the side, as well.

⅔ pound ground pork
⅔ pound ground veal
⅔ pound ground beef
1 large onion, chopped
¾ cup wheat germ
2 eggs
⅓ cup ketchup
Salt and pepper

Preheat the oven to 375°F.

Combine all the ingredients in a large bowl until the mixture holds together well. Do not overmix the meat. Turn the meat loaf mixture into a 9-inch loaf pan and smooth the top. "Frost" the meat loaf with ketchup, if desired.

Bake the meat loaf for 1 hour. Drain off the accumulated fat from the pan. Slice and serve the meat loaf.

Yield: 4 to 6 servings

VARIATIONS:
Vegetable meat loaf: Add 1 large carrot, grated; 1 medium bell pepper, cut into small cubes; and minced garlic cloves to the meat mixture.
Herbed meat loaf: Add 2 tablespoons mixed, minced green

herbs—e.g., a combination of parsley, chives, chervil, thyme, and sage—to the meat mixture.

Italian meat loaf: Add 1 cup fresh bread crumbs to the pesto-flavored meat filling in Pork Loin Stuffed with Pesto on page 154.

·:·

LAMB SAUSAGES WITH DRIED CHERRIES

Traverse City, Michigan, a lovely area in the northern "pinky" part of the Michigan mitten, is the dried cherry capital of the United States. This sausage recipe combines the delicious taste of cherries with the distinctive quality of lamb. Serve the sausages with the Bulgur Wheat Salad (page 174).

2 lengths sausage casing
½ pound boneless lamb, cut into cubes
½ pound beef chuck, cut into cubes
½ pound pork butt or shoulder, cut into cubes
¾ pound pork fat
1 tablespoon kosher salt
½ tablespoon minced garlic
½ cup dried cherries, halved or quartered if large
1 teaspoon ground cumin
½ teaspoon chili powder
Black pepper to taste

Prepare the sausage casings by first rinsing them off in cold water. Let them soak in cold water for a few minutes. Then take each casing and attach its opening to a water faucet. Turn on the tap and flush the casing with water. (If there are any holes in the casing, discard it.) Let the casings soak in fresh cool water until they are needed.

Grind the lamb, beef, pork, and pork fat through the fine blade of a meat grinder. Or process the meat in batches in the container of a food processor, using on-off pulses to start. Process the mixture until it is somewhat smooth in consistency. Add the remaining ingredients to the meat, and mix them together until they are thoroughly combined and slightly sticky.

Fry a small amount of the meat mixture in a sauté pan over medium-high heat until it is cooked through. Taste the sausage for seasoning and adjust it accordingly. Refrigerate the sausage mixture for 1 hour.

Wring out the excess water from the sausage casings. Attach one end of the sausage casing to a sausage stuffing horn or other similar device. Push the length of the casing up onto the horn but leave several inches overhanging at the end. Knot the free end and proceed to stuff the casing loosely with the sausage mixture. Form the sausages into 6-inch lengths. To do this, pinch the stuffed casing at 6-inch intervals and twist several times in opposite directions to secure each link.

Yield: 8 sausages (4 servings)

PIG BALLS STROGANOFF

New York's Coney Island area now boasts a significant population of Russian immigrants. Beef stroganoff (or stroganov) is a Russian dish dating back to the eighteenth century and named after a wealthy arts patron. Again, pork makes a delicious substitute for the traditional beef used in the recipe. You could also serve this as an hors d'oeuvre at a cocktail party.

¾ pound Swiss chard, stemmed and rinsed
Juice of ¼ lemon
½ pound ground pork
½ pound ground veal
¾ cup finely minced onion
1 large egg
⅓ cup dry bread crumbs
2 tablespoons grated Parmesan cheese
1 teaspoon salt
½ teaspoon black pepper
⅛ teaspoon grated nutmeg
¼ cup vegetable oil
2 cups Pork Stock (page 18) or beef stock
2 tablespoons butter
1 12-ounce package mushrooms, stemmed and sliced
1 tablespoon vermouth
2 tablespoons cornstarch
1 cup sour cream
Salt and pepper

Drop the chard leaves into a large saucepan containing two inches of boiling salted water mixed with the lemon juice. Cook them approximately 3 to 5 minutes, or until they are wilted but still slightly chewy. Drain the chard and run it under very cold water. Squeeze out as much excess liquid as possible from the chard and chop it finely.

Mix ½ cup chopped chard with the pork, veal, ½ cup onion, egg, bread crumbs, cheese, and spices. Combine the ingredients thoroughly but do not overmix them. Using a ⅛-cup measure, form the meat into small balls.

Heat the oil in a large sauté pan over high heat. Sauté the meatballs in batches, if necessary, to prevent overcrowding them in the pan. When nicely browned on all sides, remove the meatballs and drain them on paper towels.

Bring the stock to a boil in a Dutch oven or other heavy pot large enough to accommodate the meatballs. Add the meatballs. Reduce the heat to a simmer and cook the meatballs, covered, for 1 hour.

While the meatballs are cooking, melt the butter in a frying pan over medium heat. Add the remaining ¼ cup onion and sauté it until it becomes translucent. Next, add the sliced mushrooms and cook them until they give up their liquid. Finally, add the vermouth to the mushrooms. Turn the heat to high and boil the mushroom mixture for 1 or 2 minutes. Remove the pan from the heat and set the mushrooms aside.

When the meatballs are cooked, remove them from the stock and keep them warm. Stir ¼ cup hot stock into the cornstarch to dissolve it. While whisking constantly, add the cornstarch and sour cream to the stock. Cook the sauce over low heat until it is nicely thickened. Add the mushrooms and meatballs to the sauce and cook them over very low heat until they are heated through. Taste for salt and pepper. Serve immediately.

Yield: 4 servings

PORK AND DUCK SAUSAGES

These sausages are wonderful as a topping for pizza (page 64) or on their own served with mixed grilled or stewed vegetables.

3 lengths sausage casing
1¾ pounds duck breasts and thighs, skinned and boned
¾ pound lean pork, cut into cubes
1 pound pork fat
3 garlic cloves, minced
2 tablespoons minced shallots
1½ tablespoons salt
1½ teaspoons fennel seeds
1 teaspoon black pepper
½ teaspoon épices fines (see note)
½ cup chopped pistachios (optional)

Prepare the sausage casings by first rinsing them off in cold water. Let them soak in cold water for a few minutes. Then take each casing and attach its opening to a water faucet. Turn on the tap and flush the casing with water. (If there are any holes in the casing, discard it.) Let the casings soak in fresh cool water until they are needed.

Grind the duck, pork, and pork fat through the fine blade of a meat grinder. Or process the meat in batches in the container of a food processor, using on-off pulses to start. Process the mixture until it is somewhat smooth in consistency. Add the remaining ingredients to the meat, and mix them together until they are thoroughly combined and slightly sticky.

Fry a small amount of the meat mixture in a sauté pan over medium-high heat until it is cooked through. Taste the sausage for seasoning and adjust it accordingly. Refrigerate the sausage mixture for 1 hour.

Wring out the excess water from the sausage casings. Attach one end of the sausage casing to a sausage stuffing horn or other similar device. Push the length of the casing up onto the horn but leave several inches overhanging at the end. Knot the free end and proceed to stuff the casing loosely with the sausage mixture. Form the sausages into 5-inch lengths. To do this, pinch the stuffed casing at 5-inch intervals and twist several times in opposite directions to secure each link.

Yield: 16 sausages (4 to 6 servings)

NOTE: *Épices fines* is a spice mixture that can be purchased or made at home. Combine 1 tablespoon each bay leaves, ground cloves, ginger, mace, nutmeg, and paprika; 1½ teaspoons each cinnamon, marjoram, sage, savory, and rosemary; and ½ cup white peppercorns. Grind in a spice grinder and strain to remove any large particles. Store in an airtight jar or bag.

It has been said that when a hog is seen carrying a piece of wood in its mouth there's bad weather ahead. Others say if a hog is seen looking into the sky, the possibility of a windstorm or tornado is very good.

♦

Pork production was often referred to as a "mortgage lifter." When the going was rough, you could raise a few head of hogs to make the mortgage payments.

♦

Pigs were tamed and used as beasts of burden to pull carts.

♦

Pigs are the second most common domesticated animal next to dogs.

♦

Pigs, especially miniature breeds, make intelligent, loyal, and affectionate pets.

♦

Pigs are good swimmers. In 1954, animals on ships were anchored off the Bikini Atoll during an H-bomb test. One, Pig 311, jumped ship after the blast and swam safely to shore through the radioactive waters only to end up on display in the Washington Zoo. Even more recently, in 1984, a boy was saved from drowning by a pig named Priscilla in Houston, Texas.

Reproduced from the collections of the Library of Congress

CHOPS
AND CUTLETS

"Indian corn was the national crop, and Indian corn was eaten three times a day in another form as salt pork. The rich alone could afford fresh meat. Ice chests were hardly known. In the country fresh meat could not regularly be got, except in the shape of poultry or game; but the hog cost nothing to keep, and very little to kill and preserve. Thus the ordinary rural American was brought up on salt pork and Indian corn, or rye; and the effect of this diet showed itself in dyspepsia."

—HENRY ADAMS

Times have changed. Fresh pork products are now available virtually everywhere in this country. And of all the types of fresh pork, loin chops and cutlets are certainly among the leanest and most versatile cuts. For the true carnivore, there are inch-thick and double chops with bones to gnaw on. For the more refined diner, there are thinner-cut chops, both with and without the bone, and thin-sliced cutlets or scaloppine of pork, which cook in minutes.

The recipes in this section emphasize some of the quicker-cooking cuts of pork loin. However, you should not feel limited by these specifications. In most cases, you can substitute different cuts for others. For example, thick and thin chops are interchangeable. The only variable you need to be concerned with is cooking time. Boneless medallions make a more elegant and formal presentation than pork chops. They can be substituted in any of the recipes, too. Panfrying can be used instead of broiling or grilling. Basic procedures for plain broiled and pan-fried chops, along with approximate cooking times, have been provided as a guideline for those who wish to substitute different preparation methods. (See page 100.)

In addition to pork chops, other recipes using pork cutlets or scaloppine are included in this section. These cutlets, thin boneless slices from the loin section of the pig, need to be pounded to ¼-inch thickness for most of the recipes. To do this, place the cutlet between two sheets of waxed paper. Using the smooth side of a meat pounder, begin to pound the meat slice, moving the meat mallet from the center of the slice outward, toward its edges. Repeat this process, making sure to work the slice of meat evenly in all directions. By rotating the meat as you pound it, you will ensure a neater shape.

When using pork cutlets, always make sure to:

♦ Lubricate them well. Loin cutlets have virtually no fat. If sautéing or grilling the scaloppine, make sure your pan or grill is well oiled.

♦ Flavor them. The cutlets adapt well to marinades, which add zip to an otherwise bland cut of meat. The oil in the marinade also protects the meat from drying out during cooking.

♦ Do not overcook them. One to two minutes per side is usually adequate cooking time for such thin slices of meat.

There really is no substitute for the thin scaloppine other than equally thin slices of fresh ham, which are sometimes difficult to find.

Following are procedures for basic broiling and panfrying of pork chops. The times listed are approximate. Actual cooking times may differ depending upon individual appliances, heat sources, utensils used, and any number of variables. Chops cooked over a really hot charcoal fire may cook more quickly than chops cooked under a somewhat unreliable gas broiler. However, this should provide a general guideline for cooking. Be careful with the thinner cuts of meat that cook more quickly. There is less room for error with these.

·:·

BASIC BROILED CHOPS

For 4 chops: Combine 2 tablespoons olive oil, 1 teaspoon prepared mustard or soy sauce, a sprinkling of herbs (for example, sage, rosemary, thyme, or a combination), and salt and pepper to taste. Brush the chops lightly with the flavored olive oil and broil them until cooked through (see the time chart on page 100).

BASIC PANFRIED CHOPS

For 4 chops: Dry the chops thoroughly with paper towels and sprinkle them with pepper. Heat 2 tablespoons canola oil (or enough oil to coat the pan's surface) in a large sauté pan over high heat. (An oil like canola has a higher burning point and is therefore better suited to sautéing at high temperatures. To sauté properly, the oil must be good and hot.) Add the chops to the hot oil and sauté them according to the time chart listed below. It is preferable to turn the chops just once. If the oil begins to burn, lower the heat slightly. If the chops are to be served with a sauce, wipe out the sauté pan with a clean cloth to remove any burnt particles, if necessary, and proceed with the sauce recipe. If the oil has not burned during cooking, you can use it to sauté onions or shallots for a sauce. The browned particles will add more flavor to the finished product. Keep the cooked chops warm while you make the sauce.

APPROXIMATE COOKING TIMES

¼-inch cutlets	1–2 minutes per side
3-ounce medallions	3–4 minutes per side
5-ounce chops (½ inch thick)	5 minutes per side
1-inch-thick chops	6–7 minutes per side
1¼-inch-thick chops	8 minutes per side

PORK CHOPS À LA PUTTANESCA

This Italian "whore's style" sauce is delicious with plain roasted chops. You could substitute a roast or medallions for the chops just as easily.

3 tablespoons olive oil
1 small onion, chopped
¾ cup red wine
¾ cup water
2 garlic cloves, minced
1½ tablespoons tomato paste
1½ tablespoons Glace de Viande (page 188)
4 anchovy fillets, minced
4 tablespoons capers
¼ teaspoon dried basil
1 small bay leaf
Salt and pepper to taste
4 double-thick or 8 thin-sliced loin pork chops
Vegetable oil

Preheat the broiler or a grill.

Heat the olive oil in a sauté pan over medium heat. Add the onion and cook it until it becomes translucent. Add all the remaining ingredients except for the pork chops and vegetable oil and cook the mixture, uncovered, over medium heat until the sauce is reduced and thick enough to coat the back of a spoon, approximately 20 to 30 minutes. Remove the bay leaf.

Brush the pork chops lightly with oil and sprinkle them with salt and black pepper. Broil or grill the chops, until they are cooked approximately 7 to 8 minutes per side for the double chops and 4 to 5 minutes per side for the thinner ones.

Plate the chops and nap them with the sauce. Serve immediately.

Yield: 4 servings

PORK CHOPS WITH SWISS POTATO AND JERUSALEM ARTICHOKE STUFFING

The addition of Swiss Gruyère cheese and Jerusalem artichokes adds a different touch to a plain potato stuffing. The potato mixture can be baked separately if you do not wish to stuff the chops.

4 1¼-inch-thick pork chops
½ pound Jerusalem artichokes, peeled and cut into ¼-inch dice
1 teaspoon lemon juice
1¼ pounds white potatoes, peeled and cut into ¼-inch dice
¼ pound bacon, cut into ¼ X 1-inch strips
1 small onion, minced
2 ounces Gruyère cheese, shredded
½ teaspoon caraway seed, lightly crushed
½ teaspoon salt
¼ teaspoon dried thyme
1 cup Pork Stock (page 18) or chicken stock
Flour seasoned with salt and pepper

Butterfly the pork chops in the following manner: Using a sharp knife, slice the chops down their centers to the bone. Open up the flaps by lightly pounding them with the smooth side of a meat mallet.

Place the Jerusalem artichokes and the lemon juice in a pan with enough salted water to just barely cover the chokes. Bring them to a simmer and cook the chokes until they are almost cooked through. Drain and refresh the artichokes with cold water. Cook the potatoes in salted water until they are almost tender. Drain the potatoes.

Sauté the bacon and onion in a large ovenproof skillet over

medium heat until they are translucent and softened. Remove the bacon and onion with a slotted spoon, reserving the bacon fat, and combine them in a bowl with the Jerusalem artichokes, potatoes, and the remaining ingredients (except the stock and seasoned flour) until thoroughly mixed. Taste and adjust the stuffing for seasoning.

Preheat the oven to 325°F.

Stuff each chop with approximately ½ cup stuffing mixture. Skewer or truss the chops with toothpicks and/or string to contain the stuffing. (Any extra stuffing can be heated separately.)

Dredge the chops lightly in flour seasoned with salt and pepper. Heat the reserved bacon fat in the skillet over medium heat. Add the chops and cook them until they are nicely browned on both sides. Pour ½ cup stock into the skillet, and cover the chops with a lid or aluminum foil and bake them in the preheated oven for 1 hour. Test for doneness at this point. If the chops are cooked, remove them from the pan. If not, let them cook another 15 minutes, or until they reach the desired degree of doneness. Add the additional ½ cup stock to the pan and cook it over medium heat, stirring to scrape any browned bits from the bottom of the pan. When the sauce is slightly thickened, add the chops to the pan and turn them to coat them with the sauce. Serve immediately.

Yield: 4 servings

PORK WITH SAUCE ROBERT

Pork cutlets with sauce Robert was one of the dishes Thomas Jefferson sampled during his gustatory tour of France. Sauce Robert, a venerable sauce brune, *is considered* the *definitive embellishment for roast pork. While time consuming to make, the results are well worth the effort. Served with roasted or mashed potatoes and a selection of glazed vegetables, this classic dish makes a truly elegant—and timeless—presentation. A pork roast can be substituted for the pork chops used in this recipe.*

4 tablespoons butter
1 large celery stalk, coarsely chopped
1 large carrot, coarsely chopped
1 small onion, coarsely chopped (set aside 2 tablespoons)
3 ounces ham cut in cubes
3 tablespoons flour
3 cups brown stock or unsalted canned beef broth
1 teaspoon tomato paste
1 bay leaf
3 sprigs parsley
¼ teaspoon dried thyme
1 garlic clove, coarsely chopped
⅔ cup white wine
⅛ teaspoon black pepper
8 thin or 4 thick center-cut pork chops
Vegetable oil
Salt and pepper
Chopped parsley
24 cornichons cut into fans (for garnish)

Melt 3 tablespoons butter in a heavy saucepan over medium heat. Add the celery, carrot, onion, and ham, and sauté them until golden, approximately 10 to 15 minutes. Add the flour all at once, stirring to distribute it evenly. Continue cooking the vegetable mixture, stirring frequently, until the flour begins to brown, approximately 10 to 15 minutes. Take care not to burn the flour.

Bring the stock to a boil in a small saucepan. Add the hot stock to the vegetable and flour mixture in a steady stream, whisking continuously. Add the tomato paste, herbs, garlic, ⅓ cup white wine, and black pepper. Reduce the heat to low and simmer the sauce at least 2½ hours, preferably longer, until it is thick enough to coat the back of a spoon. Pass the sauce through a fine-mesh strainer, pressing on the solids to remove as much liquid as possible.

Sauté the reserved onion in the remaining 1 tablespoon butter until softened. Add the remaining ⅓ cup white wine. Bring the wine to a boil and reduce the mixture to approximately 2 tablespoons. Add the onion to the strained sauce and simmer for 10 to 15 minutes more. Taste and adjust for seasonings and salt.

While the sauce is cooking, preheat a broiler or grill. Coat the pork chops lightly with vegetable oil and sprinkle them with salt and pepper. Broil the chops for approximately 5 to 8 minutes per side, depending upon their thickness, or until they reach the desired degree of doneness.

Serve the pork chops with the sauce. Garnish the chops with the parsley and the cornichons.

Yield: 4 servings

PORK MEDALLIONS
IN DRIED CRANBERRY SAUCE

Cranberries are a crop almost exclusively indigenous to the United States (they are native to Russia as well), and are grown commercially in the Midwest and the Northeast—the states of New Jersey, Massachusetts, and Wisconsin account for the bulk of world production. Although they are considered unique and exotic outside of our country, the dried cranberries in this recipe add a lovely sweetness, depth, and American flavor to a very rich sauce.

4 tablespoons butter
8 3-ounce pork loin medallions
⅓ cup minced shallots
2 cups Pork Stock (page 18) or chicken stock
½ cup port
2 small sprigs thyme
1 generous teaspoon lemon rind, grated
¾ cup dried cranberries
1 cup heavy cream
1 teaspoon red currant jelly
Salt and pepper

Melt the butter in a large sauté pan over medium-high heat. Add the medallions, in batches if necessary to prevent over-crowding, and sauté them until they are cooked through and nicely browned, approximately 4 to 5 minutes per side. Transfer the medallions to a plate and keep them warm.

Add the shallots to the pan in which the medallions were cooked, and sauté them until they are softened. Scrape up any browned bits from the pan as the shallots cook.

Add the stock, port, thyme, and lemon rind to the pan. Bring the mixture to a boil and reduce it by half. Lower the heat to medium and add the cranberries. Cook the sauce until the cranberries are softened. Add the cream and currant jelly to the saucepan. Reduce the sauce over medium-high heat until it is thick enough to coat the back of a spoon. Add salt or pepper to taste.

Sauce the medallions and serve them immediately.

Yield: 4 servings

·:·

PEACHY PORK CHOPS

Here's a perfect way to use up those extra Georgia (or California or New Jersey) peaches or nectarines that have been left on the windowsill a few days too long. Make sure to use overly ripe fruit for the best flavor.

2 very ripe peaches or nectarines, peeled and finely mashed
2 tablespoons coarse-grained mustard
2 tablespoons soy sauce
1 tablespoon sherry vinegar
1 tablespoon honey
2 tablespoons safflower oil
2 garlic cloves, chopped
4 thick-cut loin pork chops

Combine all the ingredients except the pork chops in a nonreactive bowl or container. Add the pork chops and marinate, turning the chops occasionally, for several hours or overnight in the refrigerator.

Prepare a barbecue grill or preheat the broiler. Cook the

chops, approximately 7 to 8 minutes per side, or until they reach the desired degree of doneness.

Yield: 4 servings

∴

PORK WITH WILD MUSHROOM RAGOUT

This is a sinfully delicious dish. While there is no substitute for the rich earthiness of the wild chanterelles, native morels or another type of wild mushroom could be easily substituted for the chanterelles.

5$\frac{1}{2}$ ounces chanterelles or other fresh wild mushrooms
1 pound white cultivated mushrooms
4 tablespoons butter
8 3-ounce pork loin medallions
$\frac{1}{2}$ cup minced shallots
$\frac{1}{3}$ cup Madeira
$\frac{1}{3}$ cup white wine
2 to 3 teaspoons fresh thyme leaves, plus extra for garnish
$\frac{3}{4}$ cup heavy cream
Salt and black pepper

Wipe off the mushrooms with a dampened cloth to remove any dirt and cut away any tough stems. Slice or quarter the mushrooms.

Melt the butter in a large sauté pan over medium-high heat. Add the medallions, in batches if necessary to prevent over-crowding, and sauté them until they are cooked through and nicely browned, approximately 4 to 5 minutes per side. Transfer the medallions to a plate and keep them warm.

Add the shallots to the pan in which the medallions were cooked, and sauté them until they are softened. Scrape up any browned bits from the pan as the shallots cook. Add the mushrooms to the shallots, and sauté them until the mushrooms, which will release their juices and reabsorb them, are cooked through and almost dry. Be careful not to burn them. Add the Madeira, white wine, thyme, and the cream. Raise the heat to high and boil the mushroom mixture until the liquid is reduced and thick enough to coat the back of a spoon, about 10 to 15 minutes. Season with salt and pepper to taste. Spoon the sauce over the meat and garnish it with the remaining thyme leaves. Serve immediately.

Yield: 4 servings

·:·

SMOTHERED PORK CHOPS

1 tablespoon kosher salt
1 teaspoon paprika
¹/₄ teaspoon black pepper
¹/₄ teaspoon cayenne pepper
¹/₄ teaspoon white pepper
¹/₈ teaspoon garlic powder
¹/₈ teaspoon onion powder
1 cup flour
3 tablespoons vegetable oil
4 1¹/₄-inch-thick pork chops
1 cup Pork Stock (page 18) or chicken stock
2 large Vidalia or other sweet onions (for example, Maui or Walla Walla), very thinly sliced
1 cup heavy cream
Salt and pepper

Combine the salt, paprika, peppers, and garlic and onion powders in a small bowl. Add 1 tablespoon of this spice mixture to the 1 cup flour.

Heat the oil in a large sauté pan over high heat. Dredge the pork chops in the flour to coat them evenly. Add the chops to the hot oil and sauté them until they are golden brown on all sides. Lower the heat. (If there are any burnt particles on the bottom of the pan, wipe them out with a clean cloth.) Add enough chicken or pork stock to come halfway up the sides of the chops. Top the chops with the onions.

Bring the stock to a boil and simmer the pork chops and onions, covered, for 8 minutes. Turn the chops and cook them another 8 minutes. Remove the chops from the pan. Continue to cook the onions, if necessary, until they are tender.

Add the heavy cream to the pan with the onions and reduce the cream over high heat until it is thick enough to coat the back of a spoon. Season with salt and pepper to taste. Serve the creamed onions with the pork chops.

Yield: 4 servings

·:·

BENNE FILLETS

Benne is the southern word for sesame seeds, here used as a coating—along with another Dixie staple, yellow cornmeal—in this South Carolina "Low Country" recipe. The end product is crunchy and delicious and served with a sweet sauce (another southern favorite). Be careful not to burn the sesame seeds during cooking.

1 cup pork or chicken stock
⅔ cup heavy cream
1 tablespoon plum or grape jelly
1 tablespoon honey
Salt and white pepper
1 egg, lightly beaten
½ cup orange juice
⅓ cup each medium yellow cornmeal, all-purpose flour, and
    white sesame seeds
1 teaspoon salt
¼ teaspoon black pepper
1 tablespoon grated orange rind
1 pound pork scaloppine, pounded to ¼-inch thickness
2 tablespoons butter
2 tablespoons vegetable oil
1 tablespoon each fresh thyme, chopped chives, and
    julienned orange rind for garnishes

For the sauce: Combine the stock, cream, jelly and honey in a saucepan over high heat. Reduce the sauce until it is thick enough to coat the back of a spoon. Season with salt and white pepper to taste. Keep the sauce warm over very low heat.

Combine the egg and orange juice in a shallow dish, and the cornmeal, flour, sesame seeds, salt, pepper, and orange rind in another. Dip the scaloppine first in the egg mixture, coating thoroughly, and then dredge in the flour mixture until evenly coated.

Melt the butter and oil in a frying or sauté pan over medium-high heat. Sauté the fillets until they are crisp and golden, approximately 2 to 3 minutes per side, taking care not to burn the sesame seeds.

Drain the cooked fillets on paper towels. Nap them with the sauce and garnish with the herbs and orange rind. Serve immediately.

Yield: 4 servings

PORK FAJITAS

Fajitas are one of the nominally Mexican dishes that have been trans-planted to the United States—probably via California and Arizona. The recipe is very low in fat in addition to being easily prepared and fun party fare.

1/2 **cup lime juice**
2 **tablespoons tequila**
2 **teaspoons minced garlic**
2 **tablespoons olive oil**
1/2 **cup water**
2 **teaspoons salt**
1 **tablespoon sugar**
3/4 **teaspoon ground cumin**
1 1/2 **pounds pork loin fillets, pounded to** 1/4**-inch thickness**
12 **flour tortillas**
Sliced avocado
Tomato Salsa Cruda (page 173)

Combine the lime juice, tequila, garlic, olive oil, water, salt, sugar, and cumin in a nonreactive container large enough to hold all the meat. Add the fillets to the marinade, turning them so that they are evenly coated. Cover the container and let the meat marinate, refrigerated, for 5 to 6 hours.

Prepare a charcoal grill or preheat the broiler.

Remove the fillets from the marinade. Broil or grill them until they are cooked through, approximately 1 to 2 minutes per side. Slice the fillets into 1-inch strips. Serve the fajitas rolled in the tortillas with the avocado slices and salsa.

Yield: 4 servings

PORK NEGIMA-YAKI

Negima-yaki is a Japanese dish traditionally prepared with beef. However, like so many other dishes, this one works equally well with thinly sliced pork.

1 tablespoon grated ginger
3 garlic cloves, minced
½ cup soy sauce
1 cup water
¼ cup rice wine
2 tablespoons sugar
2 tablespoons honey
2 pounds center-cut pork fillets, pounded to ⅛-inch thickness
     and cut into 12 equal pieces
24 scallions, trimmed to 6-inch lengths
12 slices daikon (white radish), trimmed to ¼ X 6-inch lengths
24 toothpicks

Combine the first 7 ingredients in a small saucepan over medium heat. Swirl the pan occasionally to dissolve the sugar. Bring to a boil for 2 minutes. Remove from the heat and let the marinade cool to room temperature. Pour the cooled mixture over the pork fillets and let marinate, covered, in the refrigerator overnight or at room temperature for 2 hours.

Drop the scallions into a pan of boiling water and cook until they are slightly wilted, 1 to 2 minutes. Drain and refresh them in cold water. Set aside. Repeat this procedure for the daikon.

To assemble the *negima-yaki*: Place 2 scallions and 1 piece of daikon in the center of each fillet. Roll the fillet tightly around the vegetables to enclose them completely. Secure each roll with 2 toothpicks.

Cook the *negima-yaki* under a preheated broiler or over a charcoal grill for approximately 2 minutes per side.

Yield: 4 servings

PHILADELPHIA CHEESE "STEAKS"

The Philly cheese steak remains a culinary fixture in the City of Brotherly Love and at the boardwalks of the Jersey Shore, Philadelphia's equivalent of the Hamptons in New York. This recipe, with the distinctive substitution of pork for beef, only calls for half a pound of meat because it is designed as a luncheon dish. Quantities can be increased, if desired.

2 tablespoons butter
2 tablespoons vegetable oil
1 pound Spanish onions, very thinly sliced
¼ teaspoon dried thyme
Salt and black pepper
½ pound pork scallops, pounded paper thin
4 soft Italian rolls, split lengthwise
4 thick slices of white American cheese

Melt the butter with 1 tablespoon oil in a sauté pan over low heat. Add the onions, thyme, salt, and pepper to taste. Cook over very low heat until the onions are translucent and golden, approximately 15 to 20 minutes. Raise the heat to medium and cook, stirring frequently, until the onions are nicely browned. Set the onions aside and keep them warm.

Add the remaining 1 tablespoon oil to the pan in which the onions were sautéed. Heat it over medium-high heat. When the oil is hot, add the pork and sauté it briefly, 1 to 2 minutes per side, or until cooked through and browned.

Toast the rolls lightly under a preheated broiler. Top the bottom half of each roll with a slice of the cheese, and broil it until it is melted. Remove the roll bottoms from the oven and top them with the pork and sautéed onions. Put on tops and serve immediately.

Yield: 4 servings

PORK SCALOPPINE MILANESE

This classic method of preparing veal works well with pork. Adjust the amount of lemon juice and herbs to suit individual tastes.

½ cup flour
Salt and pepper
4 tablespoons olive oil
1 pound pork loin scaloppine, pounded to ¼-inch thickness
Juice of 1 lemon (more or less, to taste)
1 cup white wine
2 teaspoons minced garlic
2 tablespoons minced shallots
6 to 8 sage leaves, minced
1 sprig rosemary leaves, chopped
4 tablespoons butter

Combine the flour with the salt and pepper, to taste.

Heat the olive oil in a sauté or frying pan over medium-high heat. Dredge the scaloppine in the flour, shaking off any excess. (Flour the meat immediately before cooking it.) Sauté the scaloppine, in batches if necessary to prevent overcrowding, until they are golden brown, approximately 2 to 3 minutes per side. Remove the meat from the pan and set it aside.

Add 1 tablespoon lemon juice, the wine, garlic, and shallots to the pan, and cook it over medium heat while stirring to scrape up any browned bits from the pan bottom. Bring the mixture to a boil and reduce it until it becomes thickened. Reduce the heat to low. Add the herbs and swirl in the butter until it emulsifies into a sauce. Return the meat to the pan, turning it several times until it is heated through and coated with the sauce. Adjust the seasonings, and add more lemon juice, salt, and pepper, if desired. Serve immediately.

Yield: 4 servings

PORK SCALOPPINE WITH PINK GRAPEFRUIT BEURRE BLANC

Florida grapefruit with pork? Why not? This recipe is the result of an experiment to try to come up with the strangest pork coupling possible.

3 tablespoons minced shallots
3 tablespoons gin
3 tablespoons Campari
1 tablespoon grated pink grapefruit rind
⅓ cup fresh pink grapefruit juice
18 tablespoons (2¼ sticks) butter
1 pound pork loin scaloppine, pounded to ¼-inch thickness

Combine the first 5 ingredients in a small saucepan over high heat and boil the mixture until the liquid is reduced to approximately 2 or 3 tablespoons. Lower the heat to low, and whisk in 16 tablespoons butter, 1 tablespoon at a time, making sure that each piece of butter is emulsified into a thick, pale sauce before adding the next. Remove the sauce from the heat. The sauce will keep briefly on the stove, out of direct heat, or in a thermos bottle.

Melt the remaining 2 tablespoons butter in a sauté pan over medium heat. Add the pork scaloppine and sauté them until they are cooked through and browned, approximately 2 to 3 minutes per side. Serve the scaloppine with the sauce.

Yield: 4 servings

PORK STIR-FRY WITH COCONUT AND PEANUTS

This quick and easy stir-fry dish is seasoned with Thai flavorings.

1 pound pork loin scaloppine, pounded to ¼-inch thickness
2 tablespoons sesame oil
½ cup chopped onion
2 teaspoons minced garlic
1 stalk lemongrass, minced
1 1-inch piece ginger, minced
1 yellow or red bell pepper, sliced
½ cup dry-roasted peanuts
1 cup coconut milk
2 tablespoons soy sauce
¼ cup gado gado sauce or smooth peanut butter
1 teaspoon sambal oelek (red chili paste), optional
1 cup fresh mung bean sprouts

Cut the scaloppine into small pieces, approximately 1 X 2 inches long, and set them aside.

Heat the oil in a wok or stir-fry pan over high heat. When the oil is hot, add the onion, garlic, lemongrass, and ginger and cook the mixture, stirring constantly, until it becomes aromatic. Add the sliced pepper and stir-fry until soft, approximately 5 minutes. Add the pork and peanuts and toss them until the pork is cooked through and the peanuts are nicely browned.

Lower the heat and add the coconut milk, soy sauce, *gado gado* or peanut butter, and chili paste, if desired (you can add more or less). Stir the mixture until it is smooth. Taste and adjust the seasonings. Add the bean sprouts to the stir-fry and serve immediately either with an aromatic rice or over rice noodles.

Yield: 4 servings

·:·

SWEET-AND-SOUR PORK

*This dish is a Chinese-American classic, the type dished out in 1960s'
chow mein houses where they served drinks with little paper umbrellas in
them. Although this dish is normally too icky sweet for most adult palates,
this version goes easy on the sweetness. Of course, you can add more sugar
if you prefer.*

2 tablespoons peanut oil
2 tablespoons minced fresh ginger
3 garlic cloves, minced
1 onion, chopped (approximately 1¼ cups)
1¼ pounds boneless pork loin, sliced into 1 X 3-inch-long
    pieces
2 small green bell peppers, cut into cubes (approximately
    1½ cups)
½ cup tomato ketchup
¼ cup rice wine vinegar or sake
1 tablespoon sugar
2 teaspoons cornstarch
1 16-ounce can pineapple chunks packed in juice (reserve the
    juice)
White rice and steamed broccoli as accompaniments

Heat the peanut oil in a wok or deep skillet over high heat. Add the ginger and garlic and cook them, stirring frequently, until they become aromatic. Add the onion, pork, and green peppers to the wok and stir-fry the ingredients until the vegetables are softened and the pork is cooked through and no longer pink, about 5 to 7 minutes. Add the ketchup, rice wine vinegar, and sugar to the stir-fry. Lower the heat to medium and allow the mixture to cook for 2 to 3 minutes.

Dissolve the cornstarch in ¼ cup pineapple juice and add this to the pork stir-fry. Toss the ingredients until the sauce becomes slightly thickened and glossy. Add the pineapple chunks and toss until they are heated through.

Serve immediately with white rice and steamed broccoli.

Yield: 4 servings

The marvelous flavor of Virginia hams, renowned abroad since the United States began exporting them in the 1660s, was attributed to the number of snakes and acorns eaten by free-range pigs as they foraged through the woods. "Hogs are never fattened upon corn; they fatten themselves in the woods upon acorns, which, of course, is the cheapest method of producing pork and bacon. Pork and bacon fattened upon acorns is considered by many as being sweeter and better flavored than that fattened upon corn."

◆

A government decree dating from the 1800s stated that a genuine Smithfield Ham was one produced in the township of Smithfield, Virginia, from hogs raised exclusively on peanuts. The law was rescinded by a reluctant town council in 1966, due to the prohibitively high price of peanuts as feed at the time.

◆

In Colonial Williamsburg, ham, eggs, and coffee were the "Sole entertainment." It was customary in Virginia "to have a plate of cold ham on the table, and there was scarcely a Virginia lady who breakfasts without it."

◆

William Byrd held the pig in such high regard he inscribed the following in the flyleaf of his Bible: "To eat ye Ham in Perfection steep it in half Milk and half Water for thirty-six Hours, and then having brought the Water to a boil put ye Ham therein and let it Simmer, not boil, for four or five Hours according to sise of ye Ham—for Simmering brings ye Salt out and boiling drives it in."

◆

"A good Virginia Ham ought to be spicy as a woman's tongue, sweet as huh kiss, an' tender as huh love."

Crowds surround the Giant Pig "Fortune Wealth"
while a few people scramble over boulders
to reach the temple of "Fame."

HAM

"The making of a ham dinner, like the making of a gentleman, starts a long, long time before the event."

—ANONYMOUS

Ham may mean many different things to different people: glossy paper-thin slices of prosciutto over ripe melon; something in a funny shape that comes out of a can; a magnificent freshly roasted joint of meat, studded with cloves and glistening with a honey glaze. Whatever visions ham may connote, there are two basic types:

♦ Fresh Ham. The term *ham*, normally implying that a meat has been cured or preserved, is something of a misnomer when speaking about fresh ham. Fresh ham is an uncured meat product that comes from the pig's hind leg. It is generally divided into the butt and the shank portions, each weighing between seven and eight pounds. (The entire fresh ham weighs approximately fourteen pounds.)

Thin slices of fresh ham can be substituted for the ¼-inch-thick loin cutlets featured in the chapter Chops and Cutlets. They would also fill in nicely for the precooked ham steaks used in several of the recipes in this chapter. However, fresh ham, particularly in slices or small enough portions, is somewhat difficult to find. Local butcher shops can obtain fresh ham on special order given advance notice, but usually they prefer to sell fresh hams whole or in halves.

♦ Cured Ham. Originally, hams were cured—with salt, smoke, drying, or a combination of these methods—to preserve them for the winter months. The advent of refrigeration has made this preservation practice rather obsolete. However, ham is still enjoyed all over the world. Virtually every ham-making region has imparted its own special touches, in the way of seasoning and flavoring the hams during the curing process. There are two basic types of cured hams:

1. Brine or wet cured hams, injected with or immersed in a solution of water, salt, sugar, and preservatives before cooking them. Canned ham is the most common wet cured ham.

2. Dry cured hams, which are rubbed with a salt, sugar, spice, and preservative mixture and hung to dry. This drying process extracts the moisture from the meat and imparts a deeper red color to the ham. Most specialty hams—prosciutto, Black Forest, country, and other hams—are produced in this manner. Many of these products require rehydration, that is, boiling or soaking prior to cooking and serving them. Others do not.

Smoking hams in a smokehouse over a variety of woods and spices is normally accomplished after the curing process. The type of smoke—hickory versus apple wood, for example—will impart a unique flavor to the meat.

The recipes that follow incorporate a number of different hams, including whole smoked hams and country hams, cooked ham slices, and specialty hams like prosciutto and Black Forest hams. As always, feel free to improvise and experiment with different types of hams as you wish—as long as you enjoy hamming it up!

Media pigs include:

Miss Piggy, who brought French to the masses (*Moi?*)
Porky the Pig (Warner Bros. cartoon)
The Three Little Pigs (Disney cartoon)
Arnold Ziffle (two-time Patsy Award winner) of *Green Acres*
Fashion plate Noelle the Pig (*Designing Women*)

One of President George Bush's favorite foods is fried pork rinds.

In its heyday, the Short Snout Society of Greenville, South Carolina, boasted 350 members in eight states and three foreign countries. Prospective members were expected to score high on the Pig Attitude Test and pay their dues to be entitled to join the festivities at the annual Swine Ball and pig-kissing contest attended by guests in pig-appropriate outfits. Traditional fare at the galas was—what else?—pork, a practice that raised a hotly contested moral and philosophical question: Was it offensive or reaffirming to consume one's patron animal while at the same time honoring it? The debate ultimately proved divisive. Current status of the group is unknown.

COUNTRY HAM WITH
MAPLE BOURBON GLAZE

North meets South in this recipe using Kentucky bourbon and Vermont maple syrup. You can use a Smithfield or other country ham in this recipe. The Smithfield ham will have to be scrubbed with a stiff brush to remove the mold and coating from its skin. The soaking and simmering is done to remove as much of the excess salt as possible from the ham.

1 14-pound Smithfield or other country ham
1 cup maple syrup
1 cup bourbon

Scrub the ham, if necessary, to remove any mold or coating from its skin. Place the ham in a large stockpot or roasting pan and cover it completely with cold water. Let the ham soak for 2 to 3 days, changing the water every 10 to 12 hours.

Place the ham in a stockpot with fresh cold water to cover it. Bring the ham to a boil. Lower the heat and simmer the ham for 3 hours. Allow the ham to cool in the boiling water.

Preheat the oven to 300°F.

Remove the ham from the pan. With a sharp knife, remove the skin from the ham, leaving a thin layer of fat all over. Bake the ham for 3 hours.

Combine the maple syrup and bourbon in a small bowl. After the ham has baked for 3 hours, add 1 cup water to the pan and brush the ham with the maple-bourbon glaze mixture. Bake the ham another 30 minutes, continuing to baste it with the glaze every 5 minutes.

Slice and serve the ham.

Yield: Approximately 16 servings

HAM WITH FISH HOUSE PUNCH GLAZE

The Fish House, organized in 1732, was a gentlemen's fishing and cooking club officially known as the "State in Schuylkill." The club hosted floating parties and turtle feasts on barges launched in the Schuylkill and Delaware Rivers near Philadelphia. One of their most famous creations was "Fish House Punch," a concoction of cognac, rum, peach brandy, lemon, and sugar. These flavors have been combined in a glaze for a baked ham.

1 14-pound fully cooked, smoked ham
50 whole cloves (approximately)
1 cup peach preserves
¼ cup cognac
⅓ cup rum
1 teaspoon grated lemon rind
2 tablespoons lemon juice
½ teaspoon mustard powder
½ teaspoon ground ginger
1 cup white wine

Preheat the oven to 325°F.

If the ham comes with its skin attached, trim the skin from the ham, making sure to leave a layer of fat on top. Score the fat layer into diamonds, and stud the points of each diamond with a clove.

Bake the ham, scored side up, on an oiled rack set inside a roaster for 7 minutes per pound to heat it through.

While the ham is baking, combine the peach preserves, cognac, rum, lemon rind, lemon juice, mustard, and ginger in a small saucepan over low heat until all the ingredients are thoroughly combined.

Twenty minutes before the ham will finish baking, increase the heat to 425°F. Pour the white wine over the ham and brush the ham with the Fish House Punch glaze. Continue to baste the ham with the glaze and pan drippings every 5 minutes. Bake the ham until the top is browned and bubbly, which should be from 20 to 30 minutes.

Slice and serve the ham.

Yield: Approximately 16 servings

·:·

FRESH HAM WITH APPLE CIDER SAUCE

Try to get the butt end portion, which is meatier than the shank end. Have the butcher bone the ham, and remove its skin and all but a thin layer of fat. The ham should be left unrolled, because it will marinate overnight before being roasted.

1/2 fresh ham, preferably the butt portion, boned and left unrolled
1 1/2 cups white wine
2 1/2 cups apple cider
1/2 cup cider vinegar
1/2 cup Calvados or apple brandy
1 onion, sliced
2 garlic cloves, minced
1/2 teaspoon dried thyme
1/2 teaspoon dried sage
1/2 teaspoon dried rosemary

¹/₂ teaspoon black pepper
1 teaspoon dried mustard
2 tablespoons butter
2 Golden Delicious or Granny Smith apples, cored and cut
into eighths
Salt and pepper

Place the ham, unrolled, in a large nonreactive container. Combine the next 11 ingredients and pour them over the ham. Cover the dish and allow the ham to marinate overnight in the refrigerator. Turn the meat occasionally so it marinates evenly.

Preheat the oven to 400°F.

Pat the ham dry. Roll and tie the ham with butcher's twine at 1-inch intervals, and place it, seam side down, in a large roasting pan. Strain the marinade and add 3 cups liquid to the roasting pan.

Roast the ham for 15 minutes. Reduce the heat to 325°F. and continue to cook the meat, basting it frequently with the marinade, for approximately 20 minutes per pound, or until a meat thermometer inserted at the thickest point measures 145–150°F.

Let the ham rest, covered, for 15 minutes.

Melt the butter in a sauté pan over medium heat and cook the apples until they are golden brown and cooked through.

Place the roasting pan on the stove (over two burners, if necessary), and reduce the pan juices over high heat until they are slightly thickened. Scrape up any browned bits from the bottom of the roaster. Degrease the sauce and season it with salt and pepper to taste.

Slice the ham and serve it with the sautéed apple slices and pan juices.

Yield: 6 to 8 servings

BLACK FOREST HAM AND TURKEY CROQUETTES

Here's a twist on an old standby. Traditional croquettes are cone shaped. But you can form them into balls, patties, or any other shape you wish. Leftover chicken can be substituted for the turkey.

1½ cups finely minced cooked turkey
½ cup finely minced Black Forest ham
1 teaspoon minced parsley
2 teaspoons prepared mustard
3 tablespoons butter
2 tablespoons finely minced onion
4 tablespoons flour
1 cup milk
½ cup shredded Gruyère or Swiss cheese
1 egg yolk
⅛ teaspoon nutmeg
¼ teaspoon paprika
1 teaspoon salt
¼ teaspoon white pepper
1 egg, lightly beaten with a little water
2 cups fresh bread crumbs
Oil for frying

Combine the turkey, ham, parsley, and mustard in a large bowl.

Melt the butter in a small saucepan over medium heat. Add the onion and sauté it until it becomes softened and translucent. Turn the heat to high, and add the flour, all at once, to the butter. Whisk the butter and flour over high heat for approximately 3 minutes, or until it begins to turn golden colored. Add the milk to the flour mixture in a thin stream while whisking constantly. When the sauce begins to thicken, lower the heat. Whisk in the

Gruyère cheese until it is incorporated into the sauce. While whisking constantly, add the egg yolk to the sauce. Season with the nutmeg, paprika, salt, and white pepper.

Add the sauce to the turkey and ham mixture, and chill it, covered, in the refrigerator. When the mixture has cooled, divide it into 8 portions. Form each into a small cone or patty.

Heat two inches of oil in a large frying pan over high heat until it registers 350 to 360°F.

Dip each patty into the beaten egg and roll it in the fresh bread crumbs until evenly coated. Fry the patties, in batches if necessary to prevent overcrowding, until they are golden brown on all sides. Remove from the oil and let them drain on paper towels.

Yield: 4 servings

·:·

HAM PÂTÉ

A similar dish is mentioned as being served in the White House in the last century. While it does not measure up to the standards one would expect for a foreign dignitary or visiting head of state, this "pâté" is great as a canapé or spread for grilled sandwiches.

1 10-ounce piece Virginia ham
2 tablespoons mayonnaise
2 teaspoons mustard
1 teaspoon prepared horseradish
2 teaspoons dry sherry
Salt and pepper to taste
Crackers or toast points
Chopped walnuts
Sliced artichoke hearts

Grind the ham in a meat grinder or chop it very finely in a food processor using on-off pulses. Mix the ham with the mayonnaise, mustard, horseradish, and sherry, and add salt and pepper to taste.

Serve the pâté on crackers or toast points and garnish with the walnuts and artichokes, if desired.

Yield: 4 appetizer or 2 luncheon servings

·:·

HAM WITH RAISIN SAUCE

Sweet-and-sour taste combinations marry well with the flavor of ham and pork in general. This type of winy, raisiny sauce is traditionally served down South with boned, breaded pigs' feet that resemble fried chicken legs when cooked.

½ cup raisins
¾ cup dry red wine
2 tablespoons butter
2 1-pound ham slices, halved
¼ cup minced onion
1 cup Pork Stock (page 18) or chicken stock
2 tablespoons balsamic vinegar
1 teaspoon minced garlic
1 tablespoon currant jelly
1 teaspoon fresh minced rosemary leaves or ½ teaspoon dried
Salt and pepper

Combine the raisins and wine in a small saucepan over high heat. Bring the mixture to a boil for 1 minute and remove it from the heat. Let the raisins stand and macerate for 3 hours.

Melt the butter in a sauté pan over medium heat. Sauté the ham slices in the butter until they are heated through and lightly browned. Remove the ham from the heat and set it aside, covered, to keep warm. Add the onions to the sauté pan and cook them until they become translucent and golden, about 5 minutes. Add the remaining ingredients to the onions, including the wine-soaked raisins. Bring the sauce to a boil over high heat and continue cooking until the sauce is reduced by two-thirds. Taste the sauce for salt and pepper. Spoon the sauce over the ham and serve immediately.

Yield: 4 servings

∴

HAM WITH RED-EYE GRAVY

Here's a recipe for a traditional southern eye-opener—made with brewed coffee to clear the cobwebs (and red eyes—hence the name) from the previous night's festivities. While most often associated with southern cookery, a similar coffee-based sauce, flavored with cream and currant jelly and served with roasted lamb, also appears in the repertoire of Swedish cooks.

1½ tablespoons butter
2 1-pound fully cooked ham steaks, halved
½ cup green bell pepper, cut into ¼-inch dice
¼ cup minced onion
1 garlic clove, minced
1 cup freshly brewed coffee
½ Pork Stock (page 18) or chicken stock
½ teaspoon dry mustard

1 tablespoon cider vinegar
1 teaspoon molasses
1 tablespoon dry sherry
¼ teaspoon each dried thyme and oregano
Paprika, salt, and pepper, to taste
1 tablespoon arrowroot mixed with 1 tablespoon water

Melt the butter in a heavy skillet over medium heat. Sauté the ham steaks in the butter until they are heated through and lightly browned. Remove the ham from the heat and set it aside, covered, to keep it warm while preparing the sauce.

Add the green pepper and onion to the skillet and sauté them over medium heat until cooked through, approximately 5 minutes. Add all the remaining ingredients, except for the arrowroot, to the skillet. Turn the heat to high and boil the sauce for 5 minutes, or until it is reduced by half. Reduce the heat to low. Whisk in the dissolved arrowroot, stirring constantly, until the sauce is thickened and shiny looking. Adjust for seasonings to taste and serve the sauce with the ham steaks.

Yield: 4 servings

HAWAIIAN HAM STEAK

Captain Cook brought pigs to the Hawaiian Islands in 1778. In typical porcine fashion, they went native in the agreeable climate, multiplied rapidly, and became a nuisance. Pork is highly favored by Hawaiians, who will often cook a whole pig in a pit called an imu, lined with and covered by hot stones to cook the meat. The following preparation is quite simple and features what used to be Hawaii's most popular and important cash crop—the pineapple.

2 tablespoons butter
2 1-pound, fully cooked ham steaks, halved
¼ cup minced onion
½ cup red bell pepper, cut into ½-inch squares
1 teaspoon grated ginger
1 clove garlic, minced
10 ounces chopped pineapple
Salt

Melt the butter in a large sauté pan over medium heat. Sauté the ham steaks in the butter until they are heated through and lightly browned. Remove the ham from the heat and set it aside, covered, to keep it warm.

Add the onion to the pan and sauté it until it becomes translucent, approximately 3 to 5 minutes. Add the red pepper, ginger, and garlic and cook until the pepper is softened, about 5 to 7 minutes. Mix in the pineapple and cook it until it is heated through. Season the pineapple with salt to taste, and serve it with the ham steaks.

Yield: 4 servings

SHRIMP AND SCALLOPS WITH PROSCIUTTO

The versatility of ham is reflected here. Prosciutto, an Italian version of our air-cured hams, is teamed with seafood. Both shrimps and scallops are important commodities in the southern and northern states, respectively. The tradition of the American bayman, whose existence is becoming threatened, is a long one.

½ cup fresh bread crumbs
5 tablespoons butter
3 tablespoons canola or other vegetable oil
¾ pound medium shrimp, peeled and deveined
¾ pound bay scallops
3 tablespoons vermouth
Juice of 1 small lime
4 to 5 garlic cloves, minced
3 ounces prosciutto, shredded
Salt
Basic Boiled Rice (page 184)

Preheat the broiler.

Mix the bread crumbs with 2 tablespoons butter until the two are combined and formed into large crumbs. Set the crumbs aside.

Heat the oil and 3 tablespoons butter in a large sauté pan over high heat. When the fat is hot, add the shrimp and scallops and sauté them until the shrimp are pink and the scallops cooked through, about 3 to 5 minutes, depending upon the size of the seafood. Add the vermouth, lime juice, and garlic. Cook the mixture over high heat for 1 minute and reduce the heat to low. Add the prosciutto to the shrimp and scallops and taste for salt.

Divide the seafood into 4 equal portions and place each in

individual gratin dishes or other similar heatproof serving pieces. Sprinkle each dish with 2 tablespoons bread crumbs. Run the dishes under the broiler for a minute or so, or until the crumbs are browned.

Serve immediately with rice.

Yield: 4 servings

Back in Civil War days, Abraham Lincoln's body-guards were disappointed to be stationed in Washington, D.C., instead of on the war front. Lincoln remarked: "You boys remind me of a farmer friend of mine in Illinois, who said he could never understand why the Lord put the curl in a pig's tail. It never seemed to him to be either useful or ornamental, but he reckoned that the Almighty knew what he was doing when he put it there."

◆

Philip Danford Armour, progenitor of the Armour meat-packing company, was "bearish" on America. Foreseeing a Union victory (and assuming that pork prices would plummet in this eventuality after having risen consistently during the war), he began to sell pork futures at $40 per barrel as the Civil War drew to an end. By the time he was obligated to deliver the pork, for which he had been prepaid at the inflated $40 price, he was able to purchase the supply he needed to deliver for only $18 a barrel. By selling short, he reaped a tidy profit of two million dollars, an astronomical figure, particularly for that period. Armour, a great philanthropist and proponent of education, provided a rationalization for this: "I like to turn bristles, blood, bones, and the insides and outsides of pigs and bullocks into revenue now, for I can turn the revenue into these boys and girls, and they will go on forever."

◆

Eliza Leslie, a Philadelphia-based writer, declared "Pork spareribs are rarely seen on 'good' American tables." On the custom of splitting a young pig and eating its brains she says: "We have always thought it most unfeminine fancy for a lady to enjoy eating the head of anything, and the brain particularly."

Author's collection

RIBS AND ROASTS

"I well recollect cart loads upon cart loads of spare ribs, such as could not be produced elsewhere at the east . . . drawn to the water's edge and emptied into the Ohio [River] to get rid of them."

—AN ANONYMOUS JOURNALIST
Cincinnati, Ohio, 1845

"The slight sickness occasioned by eating roast pork may be prevented by soaking it in salt and water the night before you cook it."

—THE FRUGAL HOUSEWIFE, 1831

It is interesting to note how our culinary tastes have changed since the 1800s. Cuts of pork once considered waste products fit for dumping into the river as garbage or others thought to induce sickness are now considered some of the most delectable.

Recipes for roasts and ribs have been grouped together because they tend to be larger cuts of meat that require longer cooking and preparation time. (Although it is not technically a roast, one recipe for a braised shoulder or loin of pork is included as well. Recipes for roasted hams appear in the chapter on ham, pages 123–37.) Various types of ribs and roasts are presented in this section, including:

- Spareribs, which come from the belly section of the hog

- Baby back and country ribs, from the loin section

- Loin roasts: boneless, bone-in, and butterflied and stuffed

- Tenderloin roasts, the tenderest and choicest part

- A whole, roasted, stuffed, suckling pig

Some of the more dramatic presentations, like the suckling pig and crown roast of pork, are not as difficult to prepare as they would appear to be. In fact, it is the butcher who does the lion's share of the work in these cases.

However, for certain other dishes, you will have to tie the roast together with twine to help contain a stuffing or to make a neater appearance. To do this: Using a three-foot piece of butcher's twine, circle the roast lengthwise once and knot it. This is your guide line. Take the free end of the string and wrap it around the back of your hand. Twist your hand downward to make a loop of string and slip the loop over the roast. Tug gently to tighten it. Repeat this procedure, placing each new loop of twine one inch away from the previous one. Make sure the string is snug but not too tight. You want the meat to have a uniform, not bunched, appearance. When you reach the other end of the roast, wrap the twine once lengthwise around the roast and secure the string. Cut off any excess twine and proceed with the recipe. Remove the string once the roast has cooked, and use the markings to slice it.

Remember to let a cooked pork roast sit for 15 to 20 minutes before carving it to allow the juices to settle in the meat. It will keep warm for this amount of time.

∴

CARIBBEAN PORK RIBS

The Caribbean and West Indian countries were historically important in the spice trade since colonial times and even before. In fact, colonial cooks were familiar with a surprising range of "exotic" spices and flavorings, some of which are called for in this recipe. While you could substitute a domestic hot sauce for the Jamaican one in the list of ingredients, the Jamaican sauce, available from specialty and mail order companies, is more piquant and flavorful.

2½ cups pineapple juice
1 large onion, sliced
2 tablespoons Cointreau or other orange-flavored liqueur
2 tablespoons dark rum
6 tablespoons honey
2 tablespoons Jamaican hot pepper sauce (more or less, to taste)
2 teaspoons minced garlic
1 teaspoon salt
¼ teaspoon nutmeg
1 teaspoon curry powder
4 pounds baby back ribs (4 "racks")

Combine all the ingredients except for the ribs in a nonreactive container large enough to hold the meat. Reserve ⅓ cup marinade and refrigerate it. Add the ribs to the remaining marinade. Cover and let them marinate overnight in the refrigerator, turning the ribs several times to coat them evenly with the marinade.

Prepare a charcoal grill or barbecue. Cook the ribs over the hot coals, turning them occasionally and brushing with the reserved marinade until they are cooked through and crisp on the outside, approximately 15 minutes.

Serve the ribs with Jamaican hot pepper sauce on the side.

Yield: 4 servings

·:·

"JERK" PORK SPARERIBS

"Jerk" sauce, along with reggae music and Bob Marley, is a transplant from the island of Jamaica. "Jerk" houses have begun to spring up in the New York metropolitan area with the increasing presence of Jamaican immigrants and the popularity of their food. Reputedly concocted by native Arawak Indians centuries ago, "jerk" involves making a meat marinade, comprised of onions, spices, and bonnet peppers, and slow cooking. You can finish the cooking on a charcoal grill, if desired, and use boneless pork butt instead of the spareribs. "Jerk" sauce is also great on chicken.

1 pound onions, peeled and cut up
2 ounces Jamaican bonnet peppers, stemmed and seeded
2 ounces peeled gingerroot
4 garlic cloves (more or less, to taste)
1½ cups soy sauce
½ cup white vinegar
¼ cup vegetable oil
2 teaspoons ground allspice
2 teaspoons ground black pepper
1 teaspoon dried thyme, crumbled
1 teaspoon salt
1 tablespoon Jamaican hot sauce or Tabasco (more or less, to taste)
5 to 6 pounds pork spareribs (2 "racks")

Combine the onions, bonnet peppers, ginger, and garlic in the container of a food processor or blender and pulse the mixture until it is pureed. Add all the remaining ingredients, except for the spareribs, to the onion paste. Taste and adjust the sauce for seasonings.

Place the ribs in a large nonreactive container. Pour the

marinade over the spareribs, turning them to make sure they are evenly coated. Allow the ribs to marinate in the refrigerator, covered, at least 5 to 6 hours, preferably overnight.

Preheat the oven to 350°F.

Place the ribs in a large roasting pan or pot. Brush them with some of the marinade and bake them, uncovered, in the oven for approximately 2 hours, or until they are cooked through. Baste the ribs with additional marinade and turn them occasionally to ensure even cooking.

Cut the spareribs into individual ribs and serve.

Yield: 4 generous servings

PENNSYLVANIA DUTCH STUFFED SPARERIBS

A Pennsylvanian once wrote: "Probably, it is the superabundance of pork and pie the Dutch have been eating for generations that turns so many of them into walking mountains of flesh." What follows is a recipe in keeping with this Pennsylvania Dutch tradition. Bring a hearty appetite— and lots of napkins—for this one!

5 to 6 pounds spareribs (2 "racks")
⅓ cup Calvados or apple brandy
12 black peppercorns
3 allspice berries
2 cardamom pods
⅛ teaspoon ground mace
½ cinnamon stick
1 bay leaf

1 large onion, quartered
3 garlic cloves, bruised
1 cup apple butter
2½ tablespoons cider vinegar
2 tablespoons apple jelly
1 recipe Dried Apple and Prune Stuffing (page 178)

Place the spareribs in a large pot over medium heat. Add the brandy, spices, bay leaf, onion, and garlic to the pot and add enough water to cover the ribs completely. Bring the mixture to a boil. Lower the heat and allow the ribs to simmer in the broth for ½ hour. Turn the meat occasionally so that it cooks evenly. Remove the ribs from the liquid and set them aside to cool. Reserve ½ cup cooking liquid; discard the rest.

Strain the ½ cup cooking liquid and combine it with the apple butter, vinegar, and apple jelly in a small saucepan over low heat. Bring the mixture to a boil and let it cook for 5 minutes. Remove the apple butter from the heat and let it cool to room temperature.

Preheat the oven to 350°F. and lightly grease a baking dish large enough to accommodate the ribs in one layer.

To assemble the ribs: Place the ribs, meaty side down, on a work surface. Place half of the stuffing in the cavity underneath the ribs, along the bony side of the rack. Fold over the ends of the rack to enclose the stuffing. Repeat with the other rack of ribs. Place the spareribs, stuffed side down, in the oiled pan. Brush the meaty side of the ribs with a third of the apple butter mixture. Cover the pan and bake the spareribs for ½ hour. Remove the lid of the pan after the ½ hour, and brush the ribs with additional apple butter mixture. Roast, uncovered, for another ½ hour, or until the ribs are cooked through. Serve with any remaining apple butter.

Yield: 4 to 6 generous servings

TEXAS-STYLE RIBS WITH SOP AND MOP SAUCES

In this Texan barbecued rib recipe, the first sauce is a marinade in which the ribs "sop"; the "mop" sauce is a traditional tomato-based one, the kind we typically think of when barbecue sauce is mentioned. The Mop Sauce would be delicious on beef or chicken, too.

2 cups Pork Stock (page 18) or beef stock
¼ cup vegetable oil
¼ cup white vinegar
2 tablespoons prepared mustard
2 tablespoons chili powder
2 tablespoons Worcestershire sauce
2 teaspoons kosher salt
1 teaspoon paprika
1 teaspoon Tabasco sauce
1 teaspoon black pepper
1 bay leaf
2 garlic cloves, chopped
4 pounds country-style pork ribs
Texas Mop Sauce (page 192)

Combine all the ingredients (except for the ribs and the Texas Mop Sauce) in a nonreactive container large enough to hold all the meat. Taste the sop sauce for seasonings and adjust them accordingly. Add the ribs to the marinade and turn them so that they are evenly coated. Let the ribs marinate, covered, in the refrigerator for 5 to 6 hours. Bring the meat to room temperature before cooking it.

Prepare a charcoal grill and allow the coals to become very hot. Cook the ribs, basting them with the remaining marinade and turning them occasionally, until they are done, approximately 20 to 25 minutes. Serve with the Texas Mop Sauce.

Yield: 4 servings

BRAISED PORK SHOULDER

Braised pork shoulder is a homey, comforting dish perfect for an informal dinner party on a wintery day. Serve it with the Peppery Bread Dumplings with Country Ham (page 179) or boiled potatoes and steamed vegetables. If you prefer, you can use a pork loin and braise it in the oven according to the directions on page 149.

3 tablespoons vegetable oil
1 bone-in pork shoulder, approximately 3 to 4 pounds
1 large onion, coarsely chopped
2 large carrots, coarsely chopped
1 large celery stalk, coarsely chopped
Chicken or Pork Stock (page 18)
3 garlic cloves, peeled and lightly crushed
3 sprigs parsley
3 sprigs thyme
1 bay leaf
12 black peppercorns

Heat the oil in a large casserole or Dutch oven over medium-high heat. Cook the pork shoulder in the hot oil until it is nicely browned on all surfaces. Remove the pork shoulder from the pan.

Sauté the onion, carrots, and celery in the pan, scraping up any browned bits, until they are softened, approximately 10 to 15 minutes. Return the pork shoulder to the pan and add enough chicken or pork stock (or water) to come two-thirds of the way up the sides of the pork. Add the garlic, herbs, and seasonings to the pork. Bring the stock to a boil and then lower the heat. Simmer the pork, covered, turning it occasionally so that it cooks evenly. Simmer the pork until it is tender, approximately 1½ to 2 hours.

Remove the pork shoulder from the stock and let it rest, covered, to keep it warm. Bring the stock to a boil in the pan over high heat and reduce it until it is slightly thickened. Strain the sauce, pressing on the solids to extract as much juice as possible.

Cut the pork across the grain into thin slices and serve it with the dumplings and pan gravy.

Yield: 6 servings

OVEN-BRAISED PORK LOIN:
Preheat the oven to 325°F.

Substitute a 3- to 4-pound boneless loin of pork for the pork shoulder, and follow the directions up until the point where the stock is added to the casserole and brought to the simmering point. Instead of continuing to cook the meat on top of the stove, place it in the center of the oven, covered, and cook the roast for approximately 1½ hours, or until it is tender. Proceed with making the sauce in the identical manner.

Yield: 6 servings

```
┌─────────────────────────────────────────────────────┐
│                         ·:·                           │
└─────────────────────────────────────────────────────┘
```

ROAST SUCKLING PIG

This is a festive and impressive dish. Garnish the platter with greens and a small apple or orange in the pig's mouth for a dramatic presentation. Whole suckling pigs are available on special order at most butcher shops and are frequently seen at Eastertime. Have the butcher clean the pig thoroughly, inside and out.

1 10- to 14-pound suckling pig (the smaller, the better)
Salt and pepper to taste
1 recipe Corn Bread Stuffing (page 176)
4 garlic cloves, peeled and mashed into a paste
½ cup olive oil

Preheat the oven to 450°F.

Dry the pig thoroughly inside and out, and remove any stray hairs from it.

Season the inside cavity of the pig with salt and pepper. Stuff the cavity loosely with the corn bread stuffing and cook any remaining stuffing separately. Sew the stuffed cavity shut with string or truss it shut using skewers and butcher string.

Prick the pig all over its outside and rub the skin with the garlic paste. Brush the pig with the olive oil.

Place a crumpled ball of aluminum foil in the pig's mouth to keep it open and cover the ears with foil as well to prevent them from burning. Stuff the eye sockets with small balls of foil.

Place the pig on a rack in a roasting pan, belly down, with its front and hind legs extended forward. Or, if your pan and oven are not large enough to accommodate the pig in this position, place it in the roaster with its forelegs bent back. Skewer the front and back legs of the pig and tie them to the rack to secure the pig while it roasts. Tuck the tail of the pig into the rear opening to prevent it from burning.

Roast the pig for 15 minutes. Baste the pig with oil and reduce the heat to 350°F. Roast the pig for approximately 2½ to 3 hours, basting it every 20 minutes with the pan drippings or additional olive oil. The pig is cooked when it has reached an internal temperature of approximately 160°F., the thigh meat feels soft to the touch, and the legs move easily in their sockets. Allow the pig to rest 20 to 30 minutes before carving.

Make a sauce from the pan drippings (page 189).

Yield: 10 to 12 generous servings

∴

"CELESTIAL" ROAST PORK

Celestials was the name given to early immigrants who, captivated by gold fever in 1852, made the trans-Pacific voyage from China to the California gold fields. (Celestial refers to the Celestial Empire, China's old name.) Their American dream was soon shattered, however. Relegated to only the poorest mining sites and shunned by society at large, many Celestials were forced to find other means to survive, for example, by opening restaurants or becoming laborers. It was in California during this period that the first chop suey houses appeared. Because traditional Chinese sauces were expensive to prepare and authentic ingredients hard to obtain, the Celestials became masters of adaptation. By incorporating local ingredients in their native cuisine, they created a unique style of cookery that was much admired and enjoyed. This recipe, and others, is a tribute to them.

1 3½-pound sirloin roast, boned, rolled, and tied
2 to 3 garlic cloves (more or less to taste), slivered
1 tablespoon mustard

¼ cup maple syrup

2 tablespoons bourbon

Juice of 1 lemon

1 teaspoon ginger juice (squeezed from grated ginger)

2 tablespoons safflower oil

1 tablespoon soy sauce

1¼ teaspoons Chinese five-spice powder (see note)

¼ teaspoon each salt and pepper

1 stalk celery

1 onion

1 carrot

1 apple

2 cups reduced pork or chicken stock

Make small incisions in the roast and insert the garlic slivers into them. Set the roast aside.

Make the marinade by combining the next nine ingredients in a nonreactive dish or container and pour the marinade over the roast, turning to coat it evenly. Cover and refrigerate the roast overnight, and turn it in the marinade occasionally.

An hour before cooking, bring the roast to room temperature. Preheat the oven to 350°F.

Coarsely cut up the celery, onion, carrot, and apple, and scatter them over the bottom of the roasting pan. Place the roast on top of the vegetables and pour the remaining marinade into the pan. Cook the roast for approximately 1½ hours to 1¾ hours, basting with the pan juices every 20 to 30 minutes, or until a meat thermometer registers the desired degree of doneness (145 to 150°F.). Place the roast on a cutting board and let it rest for at least 10 minutes before slicing.

Meanwhile, pour the contents of the roasting pan through a strainer, pressing on the solids to extract as much juice as possible. Return the liquid to the roasting pan and add the stock. Bring the sauce to a boil on top of the stove and scrape up any brown bits from the pan. Reduce the liquid over high heat until the pan juices are slightly thickened.

Slice the pork and serve it with the sauce.

Yield: 4 to 6 servings

NOTE: Chinese five-spice powder is equal parts Szechuan pepper-corns, star anise, fennel, cinnamon, and cloves.

∴

CROWN ROAST OF PORK WITH MINTED PAN GRAVY

This impressive-looking main course is actually rather easy to make. It involves cooking time in the oven and making a simple pan gravy at the end. The crown roast would look lovely with any of the vegetable purees spooned into the center and garnished with sprigs of fresh mint or rosemary.

1 8-pound crown roast of pork
2 garlic cloves, cut in half
¼ cup vegetable oil
2 tablespoons soy sauce
2 tablespoons honey
1 tablespoon prepared Dijon mustard
1 teaspoon chopped fresh rosemary
1 teaspoon chopped fresh mint
Salt and pepper
Pan Gravy (page 189)

Preheat the oven to 375°F.

Rub the meat with the cut sides of the garlic cloves. Combine the oil, soy sauce, honey, mustard, and herbs. Brush the roast, inside and out, with the oil mixture and sprinkle it with salt and pepper.

Place the roast on a rack inside a roasting pan. Cook the roast, basting it with the accumulated pan juices every half hour, for approximately 2 hours, or until a meat thermometer inserted in the center of the meat registers 150°F. Remove the crown roast from the oven, tent it with foil, and allow it to rest at room temperature for 15 to 20 minutes before carving.

Garnish the roast and cut it into individual ribs at tableside. Serve with the Pan Gravy.

Yield: 8 servings

∴

PORK LOIN STUFFED WITH PESTO

The pesto craze of the '70s and '80s was a phenomenon emanating from California and the "California cuisine" movement. This recipe combines that somewhat-forgotten taste sensation with spinach. There is no need to relegate this delicious filling to playing second fiddle—it makes a wonderful meat loaf, too! See page 87 for a recipe using these ingredients.

1 10-ounce package frozen leaf spinach, defrosted
¾ pound ground pork
½ cup chopped onion
¼ cup Pesto Sauce, preferably homemade (page 191)
2 tablespoons grated Romano cheese

2 tablespoons grated Parmesan cheese
1 teaspoon minced garlic
Salt and pepper
1 3½-pound sirloin roast, boned and butterflied to ½-inch
        thickness
Vegetable oil

Preheat the oven to 375°F.

Defrost the spinach. Squeeze out as much excess water from the defrosted spinach as possible and chop it finely. Combine the spinach with the ground pork, onion, pesto, cheeses, garlic, salt, and pepper.

Sprinkle the inside of the meat with the salt and pepper and spread the filling evenly over the meat, leaving a ½-inch border all around. Roll the meat to completely enclose the filling and tie the roast at 1-inch intervals with butcher's string. Coat the roast lightly with vegetable oil and sprinkle it with salt and pepper. Place the loin in a roasting pan in the preheated oven and cook it for 45 minutes, or until the desired degree of doneness is reached. Slice and serve immediately.

Yield: 4 servings

ROLLED LOIN OF PORK WITH FENNEL AND RED PEPPER

The Italian-style stuffing for this roast would be a tasty side dish on its own. But its contrasting colors, textures, and flavors make a colorful presentation as a stuffing.

2 tablespoons butter
½ cup chopped onion
1 large fennel bulb, cut into ¼-inch dice (approximately 2 cups)
1 large red bell pepper, cut into ¼-inch dice (approximately 1 cup)
2 teaspoons minced garlic
¼ pound fontina cheese, cubed
2 cups cooked rice
Salt and pepper to taste
1 3-pound sirloin roast, boned and butterflied to ½-inch thickness
Vegetable oil

To prepare the filling: Melt the butter in a large skillet over medium heat. Add the onion and fennel and cook, covered, for 15 minutes, or until the onion is softened and golden. Add the red bell pepper and garlic and continue to cook for 5 minutes more. Mix together the vegetables with the fontina cheese and rice. Season with salt and pepper to taste and cool the rice filling to room temperature.

Preheat the oven to 375°F.

Sprinkle the inside of the meat with salt and pepper. Spread the cooled filling over the meat, leaving a ½-inch border all around. Roll the meat to completely enclose the rice mixture and tie the roast at 1-inch intervals with butcher's string. Lightly coat the meat with vegetable oil and sprinkle it with salt and pepper. Cook the roast for 45 minutes, or until the desired degree of doneness is reached. Slice and serve the roast immediately.

Yield: 4 to 6 servings

·:·

NORTH CAROLINA BARBECUED TENDERLOIN

Sarah Hicks Williams, a New York woman who emigrated to North Carolina in 1852 to live on her husband's family plantation, wrote about southern cuisine in a letter to her parents: "Red pepper is much used to flavor meat with the famous 'barbecue' of the South and [the dish] which I believe they esteem above all dishes is roasted pig dressed with red pepper and vinegar." Here is a modern version of this North Carolina "barbecue." The tenderloin is marinated in a spice mixture, barbecued over hot coals, and served, sliced, in lettuce leaves with a vinegar and red pepper dressing.

SPICE RUB

1 tablespoon kosher salt
1 tablespoon granulated sugar
1 tablespoon brown sugar
1 teaspoon chili powder
1 teaspoon ground cumin
1 teaspoon hot paprika
¼ teaspoon black pepper
¼ teaspoon cayenne pepper

¼ teaspoon white pepper
⅛ teaspoon garlic powder
⅛ teaspoon onion powder

2 pork tenderloins (approximately 1¼ pounds)
1 head Boston lettuce, separated into leaves and washed
Vinegar BBQ Dressing (page 193)

Combine all the ingredients for the spice rub and mix them together thoroughly. Rub the spice mixture over the surface of the tenderloins to coat them evenly. Let the tenderloins sit, covered, in the refrigerator for 5 to 6 hours. Bring the meat to room temperature before cooking it.

Prepare a charcoal grill and allow the coals to get very hot. Cook the tenderloins over the coals, turning them occasionally, for approximately 25 minutes, or until they reach a desired degree of doneness.

Thinly slice the tenderloins and serve the slices wrapped in the lettuce leaves with the Vinegar BBQ Dressing as a condiment.

Yield: 4 servings

PORK TENDERLOIN IN SHERRY-MUSTARD CREAM SAUCE

This is an easy yet elegant main dish to prepare. Make the sauce while the tenderloins are roasting in the oven, and be sure to serve them with lots of bread, potatoes, or rice to soak up the extra sauce.

2 pork tenderloins (approximately 1¼ pounds)
1 tablespoon butter
1 tablespoon vegetable oil
1 small onion, minced
½ cup dry Fino sherry
1 cup Pork Stock (page 18) or chicken stock
1 cup heavy cream
2 tablespoons coarse, country-style Dijon mustard
¼ teaspoon dried tarragon, crumbled
Salt and pepper to taste

Preheat the oven to 375°F.

Dry the tenderloins with a paper towel. Melt the butter with the oil in a large sauté pan over medium-high heat. Add the tenderloins to the hot oil and sauté them until they are nicely browned all over. Transfer the tenderloins to a roasting pan and roast them until they are cooked, 20 to 25 minutes.

Add the onion to the sauté pan in which the tenderloins were browned. Cook it, scraping up any browned bits from the bottom of the pan, until the onion becomes translucent. Turn the heat to high and add the sherry, stock, and heavy cream. Reduce the sauce until it becomes thick enough to coat the back of a spoon. Lower the heat and add the mustard, tarragon, and salt and pepper to taste.

Slice each pork tenderloin into 8 pieces. Add the pieces to the sauce, along with any accumulated juices, and turn them in the sauce until they are well coated. Serve immediately.

Yield: 4 servings

TENDERLOIN AU POIVRE

Not for the fainthearted, this dish is very spicy.

2 1-pound pork tenderloins
3 tablespoons vegetable oil
4 tablespoons minced shallots
4 tablespoons black peppercorns, cracked
3 tablespoons coarse-grained Dijon mustard
5 tablespoons sour cream or crème fraîche
2 teaspoons prepared horseradish (more or less, to taste)
½ cup fresh bread crumbs

Preheat the oven to 375°F.

Trim any small ends from the tenderloins so that they are of uniform thickness.

Heat the vegetable oil in a sauté pan over high heat. When the oil is hot, add the tenderloins and sear them until they are browned all over, approximately 5 to 7 minutes. Remove the tenderloins from the heat and set them aside on a clean work surface.

Combine the remaining ingredients to form a thick paste. Coat the tops and sides of the tenderloins evenly with the bread crumb mixture. Transfer the tenderloins to a shallow baking pan and roast them in the preheated oven for 20 to 25 minutes, or until a meat thermometer registers 145 to 150°F. Remove the meat from the oven and slice it into medallions. Serve immediately.

Yield: 6 servings

PIG PUZZLER

Match the following with their meaning.

1. Pig wife
2. Pig in a poke
3. Like a hog in harvest
4. Hog shearing
5. Hog on ice
6. St. Bartholomew Pig
7. To bring home the bacon
8. To drive a hog to market
9. Pigtail
10. Pig's ear
11. To baste bacon
12. A still sow
13. To eat Dunmow Bacon
14. To go to pigs and whistles
15. St. Anthony's Pig
16. Hog
17. Pig puzzle
18. Piggywhidden

a. runt of the litter
b. cocky, self-assured, confident
c. beer
d. to be ruined
e. a blind bargain
f. shilling, sixpence
g. to snore loudly
h. in one ear, out the other
i. to live in marital bliss
j. a type of tobacco
k. a very fat person
l. a selfish person
m. a crockery vendor
n. to thrash
o. to catch a greased pig
p. much ado about nothing
q. fairy, elf
r. a gate made to swing both ways

ANSWERS: 1m; 2e; 3h; 4p; 5b; 6k; 7o; 8g; 9j; 10c; 11n;
12l; 13i; 14d; 15a; 16f; 17r; 18q.

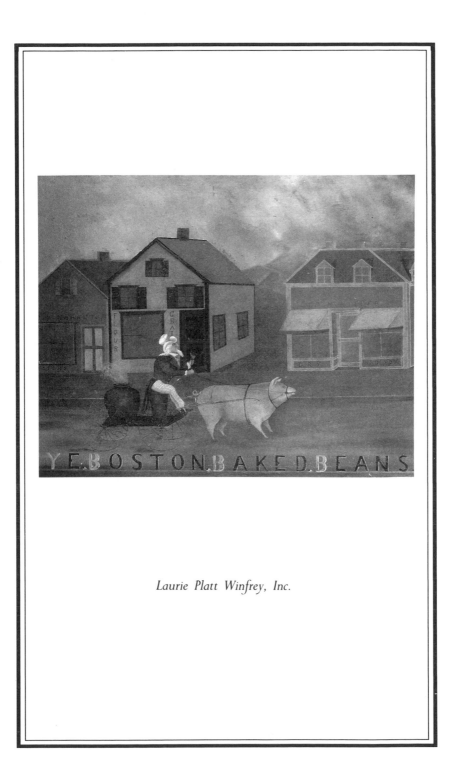

Laurie Platt Winfrey, Inc.

ACCOMPANIMENTS

"It was Cincinnati which originated and perfected the system which stuffs fifteen bushels of corn into a pig and packs that pig into a barrel, sending him over the mountains and across the seas to feed mankind."

—ANONYMOUS

In this section, vegetables like corn will play a slightly different role than in the quote above.

Included are recipes for vegetables and starchy accompaniments (potatoes, rice, bread stuffings, and other grain-based dishes) as well as recipes for miscellaneous sauces and dressings. Several have been designed specifically to go with individual recipes appearing throughout the book. Others have been conceived as side dishes appropriate to serve with pork or other main course meat dishes. Whichever of the accompaniments you choose to make, there are a few pointers you should keep in mind:

- The elegant yet simple vegetable purees can be whipped up with little fuss. However, those made from potatoes should *never* be prepared in a food processor, which will yield a gummy, sticky mess. A potato masher, food mill, or ricer is the implement of choice for preparing any potato-based or other highly starchy vegetable puree (beans, for example). A food mill, though it requires a bit of elbow grease, generally yields finer, more uniform results for pureed dishes.

♦ When cooking rice, the most important thing is: Let it alone. Do not peek into the pan while the rice is cooking. Do not lift the cover of the pan. Do not stir the rice. If you allow it to sit undisturbed as it cooks, the rice will come out perfect. Although there are several ways to determine the amount of water to be used when cooking rice, a good guideline is 1 part rice (dry measure) to 1½ parts water (liquid measure). If for some reason there is excess water in the rice after it has cooked the required amount of time, either drain off the water or allow the rice to simmer, uncovered, until the water has evaporated.

♦ When making glazed vegetables, try to keep the vegetables uniform in terms of size and shape. This will ensure both a better final presentation and more evenly cooked vegetables.

BRAISED RED CABBAGE

Sarah Kemble Knight described a dish of pork and cabbage she was served at an inn in 1704: "The sause was of a deep Purple, wch I th't was boil'd in her dye Kettle; the bread was Indian, and . . . I being hungry, gott a little down; but my stomach was soon cloy'd, and what cabbage I swallowed serv'd me for a Cudd the whole day after." This naturally purple cabbage, teamed with Bratwurst (page 76), assuredly will go down easier than the dinner described above.

2 tablespoons butter
1 large onion, thinly sliced
2 small tart apples, thinly sliced
½ large red cabbage, thinly sliced
⅓ cup sherry vinegar
3 tablespoons blueberry vinegar
Juice of ½ lemon
½ cup water
6 whole cloves
6 juniper berries
1 cinnamon stick
¼ cup brown sugar
½ cup raisins
2 teaspoons salt

Melt the butter in a large saucepan or Dutch oven over medium heat. Add the onions and apples and cook them, covered, approximately 15 minutes, or until they become golden and translucent. Add the cabbage and the remaining ingredients, and continue to cook the vegetables, covered, over very low heat for at least 2½ hours, preferably 3 to 4 hours. Remove the cloves, juniper berries, and cinnamon before serving.

Yield: 4 to 6 servings

CREAMED COLLARDS AND KALE

Nobody will refuse to eat their greens in this form. The cream added at the end of the recipe makes the collards and kale especially rich. It can be left out, if desired.

1 small bunch kale (approximately 1 pound)
1 large bunch collards (approximately 2 pounds)
Juice of ½ lemon
Salt and white pepper
2 tablespoons butter
1 large onion, chopped
4 slices bacon, cut into ¼ X 1-inch strips
½ teaspoon thyme
1½ pints heavy cream

Separate the leaves from the tough stalks on the greens and wash them thoroughly. Add the lemon juice and 1 tablespoon salt to 4 quarts water. Bring the water to a boil. Blanch the greens by dropping them into the rapidly boiling water. Cook them approximately 10 to 15 minutes, or until they are soft but slightly underdone. (They will receive additional cooking time at the last minute.) Drain and refresh the greens with cold water. When cool enough to handle, squeeze out the excess water from the greens and chop them. (The recipe can be prepared ahead until this point.)

Melt the butter in a heavy sauté pan over medium heat. Add the onion, bacon, thyme, and pepper to taste, and cook the mixture over low heat until it is softened and translucent but not browned. Add the cream and bring the sauce to a boil. Reduce the cream until it is thickened. Lower the heat and add the chopped greens. Simmer the vegetables until they are heated through. Taste for salt and pepper. Serve immediately.

Yield: 6 to 8 servings

∴

GINGERED CARROT PUREE

This puree would look beautiful spooned inside the Crown Roast of Pork with Minted Pan Gravy (page 153) or served with plain broiled pork chops or baked ham.

3 tablespoons butter
8 large carrots, sliced into 1/4-inch rounds
1 2-inch piece ginger, peeled and thinly sliced
2 small onions, thinly sliced
1/4 cup chicken stock
Salt and pepper to taste
Chives, to garnish

Melt the butter in a medium saucepan over low heat. Add the carrots, ginger, onion, and chicken stock to the pan. Cover the vegetables with a buttered round of wax paper and cook them over low heat until they are tender, approximately 1/2 hour.

Puree the vegetables in the container of a food processor or pass them through the fine blade of a food mill. Add salt and pepper to taste, and additional chicken stock if necessary to thin the puree. Garnish the puree with chopped chives and serve immediately.

Yield: 4 to 6 servings

GLAZED VEGETABLES

Glazed vegetables are a simple yet elegant accompaniment for roasted meats. This technique will work well with any type of root vegetable— carrots, onions, beets, turnips, parsnips, and celery root, to name a few. You can slice the vegetables or carve them into five- or six-faced football shapes, the classic "turned vegetables" of French cooking. (If you decide to turn the vegetables, remember there is a lot of waste with this particular method of preparation. You may need more vegetables to account for this. Use the scraps in soups or stocks.) Just be sure that the vegetables are of equal thickness, whatever the shape.

1½ to 2 pounds vegetables, cut into pieces of equal thickness
4 tablespoons butter
2 tablespoons sugar
Salt

Place the vegetables, butter, and sugar in a pot large enough to accommodate them in a single layer and sprinkle them with salt. Add ½-inch water to the pan. Bring the water to a simmer over a very low flame, and cook the vegetables, covered, until they are tender and the water has evaporated. If the vegetables start to burn, add a little more water. The cooking should take up to 1 hour, depending on the size of the vegetables. Remember to shake the pan and roll the vegetables around a bit while they cook to ensure better glazing.

Yield: 4 to 6 servings

GRATIN OF ZUCCHINI AND EGGPLANT

This recipe can be made using either Italian Ragu (page 52) or a ready-made sauce. If any extra water from the zucchini accumulates in the pan as the gratin cooks, just drain it off.

¾ pound zucchini, sliced into ¼-inch rounds
¾ pound baby eggplant, very thinly sliced lengthwise
Salt
Vegetable oil
2½ cups Italian Ragu (page 52) or spaghetti sauce
¼ cup heavy cream
½ pound mozzarella cheese, coarsely grated
2 ounces Parmesan cheese, grated

Place the zucchini and eggplant in separate colanders or strainers. Sprinkle the vegetables with salt and toss to coat them evenly. Let the zucchini and eggplant drain for 2 hours at room temperature.

Preheat the oven to 375°F. and lightly grease an 8-inch square pan with the vegetable oil.

Combine the ragu with the heavy cream.

Squeeze out as much water as possible from the eggplant and zucchini. Lay half the eggplant slices, overlapping them, to cover the bottom of the pan. Spread 1 cup ragu cream sauce over the eggplant, and spread half the zucchini on top of the sauce. Cover the zucchini slices with half the mozzarella and Parmesan cheeses. Repeat this layering process again, and top the gratin with the remaining ragu cream sauce.

Bake the gratin in the preheated oven for approximately 30 to 40 minutes, or until it is bubbling and the vegetables are cooked through.

Yield: 4 servings

MASHED TURNIPS WITH CARAMELIZED SHALLOTS

These are not the mashed turnips your grandmother forced you to eat as a child. Even the most inveterate vegetable hater will be asking for a second helping of these.

1¾ pounds rutabaga (yellow turnip), peeled and cut into pieces
½ pound white potatoes, peeled
6 tablespoons butter
6 ounces shallots, peeled and thinly sliced
½ cup heavy cream
1½ teaspoons salt

Place the rutabagas and potatoes in separate saucepans with enough salted water to just barely cover them. Bring them to a boil, partially covered, over medium heat, and simmer the vegetables until they are tender, approximately 30 to 45 minutes.

While the turnips and potatoes are cooking, melt 2 tablespoons butter in a sauté pan over low heat and sauté the shallots, stirring them occasionally, until they are golden brown in color. This should take approximately 25 to 30 minutes.

Drain the turnips and potatoes, and pass them through the fine blade of a food mill along with the sautéed shallots (you can reserve some of the shallots for a garnish if you wish). Mix the vegetable puree thoroughly and return it to the sauté pan.

Before serving, heat the turnips over low heat. Add the remaining butter, the cream, and the salt to the vegetables. Stir the mixture frequently to prevent sticking and to incorporate the butter.

Yield: 4 to 6 servings

TOMATO SALSA CRUDA

The salsa is a perfect accompaniment to Pork Fajitas (page 112). However, it would go well with the Corn Cakes with Ham (page 175) also. Just be sure to use the most flavorful, ripest tomatoes available.

1 large tomato, chopped (approximately 1 cup)
1½ tablespoons minced onion
1 stalk celery, finely minced (approximately ¼ cup)
1 tablespoon chopped fresh basil
1 teaspoon chopped fresh coriander (cilantro)
½ teaspoon salt

Combine all the ingredients in a small nonreactive bowl or container. Taste the salsa and adjust for seasonings. Cover and refrigerate the tomato mixture for several hours to combine the flavors.

Yield: 4 servings

BULGUR WHEAT SALAD

Serve this salad with the Lamb Sausages with Dried Cherries on page 88.

4 cups water
1½ teaspoons salt
1½ cups bulgur wheat
1 large tomato, diced
3 green onions, sliced
⅓ cup vinaigrette dressing
1 tablespoon chopped parsley
Salt and pepper to taste

Bring the water and the salt to a boil in a medium saucepan. Add the bulgur wheat. Reduce the heat and simmer the wheat, covered, for 10 minutes. Remove the bulgur wheat from the heat and let it sit for 15 minutes. Drain the bulgur wheat very thoroughly and allow it to cool to room temperature. Mix in the remaining ingredients.

Yield: 4 to 6 servings

CORN CAKES WITH HAM

This recipe is really a cross between an Italian polenta and a southern corn mush or corn pudding. Its mild flavors would contrast well with a spicy salsa or a rich gravy served on the side. It can be prepared a day or two ahead and grilled to heat it through at the last moment.

2 tablespoons butter
¼ cup minced onion
5 ounces ham, cut into ½-inch cubes
Pinch of dried thyme
1 garlic clove, minced
3½ cups water
1½ teaspoons salt
1¼ cups yellow cornmeal
2 eggs
½ cup grated Parmesan cheese
½ cup corn kernels
Melted butter

Preheat the oven to 350°F. and grease an 8-inch square baking pan.

Melt the butter in a small sauté pan over medium heat. Add the onion and sauté it until it becomes translucent and golden. Add the ham, thyme, and garlic and cook until the ham is lightly browned. Remove the pan from the heat and set it aside.

Bring the water with the salt to a boil in a medium saucepan. Add the cornmeal in a thin slow stream while stirring constantly to prevent lumps from forming. Reduce the heat and cook the mixture until the cornmeal becomes thick and begins to pull away from the sides of the pan, approximately 10 minutes. Remove the cornmeal from the heat and add the eggs one at a time, stirring constantly with each addition to prevent the eggs from curdling. Add the Parmesan cheese, corn, and ham mixture and stir well to incorporate the ingredients.

Turn the cornmeal into the greased baking pan. Smooth the top as much as possible. Cover the corn pudding with aluminum foil and bake it, covered, for 30 to 35 minutes, until it is light and fluffy and a knife inserted into it comes out clean. Let the corn pudding cool at room temperature and then refrigerate it overnight.

To serve: Preheat the broiler or prepare a barbecue grill. Cut the pudding into squares and brush them on both sides with the melted butter. Broil or grill the squares until they are lightly browned and heated through, approximately 2 to 3 minutes per side.

Yield: 4 servings

·:·

CORN BREAD STUFFING

This recipe will make enough to stuff the Roast Suckling Pig (page 150)—and then some! Any leftover or extra stuffing can be cooked in a separate pan or casserole as the pig roasts. This stuffing would also be lovely mounded into the Crown Roast of Pork with Minted Pan Gravy (page 153). Just use half the quantity of stuffing.

9 slices white or whole wheat bread, cut into 1-inch cubes (approximately 5 cups)
4 cups corn bread crumbs, preferably homemade
1 pound sage-flavored sausage, preferably homemade
8 tablespoons butter

3 stalks celery, minced
2 medium onions, minced
12 ounces mushrooms, stemmed and sliced
2 apples, cut into small chunks
1 cup raisins
½ cup chopped walnuts
1 teaspoon salt
1 teaspoon black pepper
½ teaspoon dried thyme
½ teaspoon dried marjoram
1 cup Pork Stock (page 18) or chicken stock

Spread the bread cubes and crumbs on a cookie sheet in a single layer and bake them in a 300°F. oven until they are lightly toasted but not browned, about 15 minutes. Remove them from the oven and place them in a large mixing bowl.

Cook the sausage in a large sauté pan over medium heat, breaking up the meat as it cooks. When the sausage is cooked through and no longer pink, remove it from the pan with a slotted spoon and let it drain on paper towels.

Melt the butter in a sauté pan over medium heat. Add the celery and onions and cook them until they are softened and translucent, 8 to 10 minutes. Add the mushrooms to the pan and sauté them until they are cooked through. Add the apple chunks to the pan and toss to coat them with the butter.

Add the celery and onion mixture, the sausage, raisins, and walnuts to the bread cubes along with the seasonings. Add almost all the stock to the stuffing mixture and stir until it is well moistened but not wet. (You may need to add a bit more water or stock, depending on how dry the bread was.) Taste and adjust for seasoning.

Yield: 10 to 12 servings

DRIED APPLE AND PRUNE STUFFING

This stuffing was designed for use with the Pennsylvania Dutch Stuffed Spareribs (page 145). However, it would be equally delicious served as a side dish, used in stuffed pork chops, or as a traditional-style stuffing for a Thanksgiving turkey.

18 large prunes, pitted
2 tablespoons Calvados or apple brandy
1½ cups dried apple slices
18 slices firm-textured white bread, cut into 1-inch cubes
     (9 cups)
6 tablespoons butter
3 stalks celery, minced (approximately 1 cup)
1½ cups minced onion
1 teaspoon salt
1 teaspoon black pepper
¾ teaspoon powdered sage
¾ cup water

Preheat the oven to 300°F.

Cut the prunes into sixths (there should be about 1 cup) and combine them with the Calvados. Cut the apple slices into smaller, bite-sized pieces.

Spread the bread cubes on a cookie sheet in a single layer and bake them in the oven until they are lightly toasted but not browned, about 15 minutes. Remove them from the oven and place them in a large mixing bowl.

Melt the butter in a sauté pan over medium heat. Add the celery and onion and cook them until they are softened and translucent, 8 to 10 minutes.

Add the celery and onion mixture, the prune mixture, and the apples to the bread cubes along with the salt, pepper, and sage. Add the water and stir until the stuffing mixture is well moistened but not wet. (You may need to add a bit more water, depending on how dry the bread was.) Taste and adjust for seasoning.

Yield: 4 to 6 servings

PEPPERY BREAD DUMPLINGS WITH COUNTRY HAM

This spicy dumpling mixture could be used as a bread stuffing for a roast or baked in the oven as a side dish as well. It is based upon a recipe for dumplings served with Philadelphia pepper pot, attributed to one of General George Washington's army cooks who cobbled it together from scraps in his kitchen during the Battle at Valley Forge. This recipe does not include tripe, a traditional ingredient for pepper pot. But if you have leftover tripe scraps, you can substitute them for the country ham in the recipe.

½ pound ground pork
¼ cup finely minced onion
3 tablespoons dry sherry
6 cups fresh bread crumbs
½ cup shredded or minced country ham
½ teaspoon dried marjoram, crumbled
½ teaspoon dried thyme, crumbled
¼ teaspoon ground cloves
1 teaspoon black pepper
1 teaspoon salt
2 eggs

Sauté the pork and the onions together in a nonstick skillet over medium heat. When the pork is almost completely cooked through, add the sherry. Turn the heat to high and boil the mixture for 2 minutes. Add the pork and onions to the bread crumbs, along with the remaining ingredients except for the eggs. Taste the stuffing for seasonings and add the eggs.

Bring an inch of water to a boil in a large pan that can accommodate a steamer. Using ¼-cup measure, shape the stuffing mixture into 16 dumplings. Place the dumplings in the steamer and cook them, covered, for 20 minutes.

Yield: 6 to 8 servings

·:·

GRUNT WITH A THOUSAND

Aka Boston baked beans, the name for this dish comes from (of all places) the movies, specifically an old silent film starring Fatty Arbuckle, in drag, as a short order cook. One of his orders is for "grunt with a thousand on a plate," which, we are shown, is pork and beans. True to the tradition of New England pork cookery, these beans are merely flavored with pork.

2 cups navy beans
1 ham hock
1 onion, cut in half
2 garlic cloves bruised
½ bay leaf
2 ounces salt pork
1 cup ketchup
1 tablespoon Dijon mustard

1 tablespoon molasses
2 tablespoons brown sugar
2 tablespoons maple syrup
Salt and pepper to taste

Rinse the beans in cold water and remove any foreign objects from them. Place the beans in a medium saucepan with 4 cups water. Bring the beans to a boil for 2 minutes. Remove them from the heat and let the beans sit, covered, for 2 hours.

Add the ham hock, half the onion, the garlic, bay leaf, and an additional cup of water to the beans. Bring them to a boil. Reduce the heat and let the beans simmer, uncovered, for approximately an hour, or until they are just tender.

Preheat the oven to 325°F.

While the beans are cooking, cut the salt pork into slices ¼-inch thick and mince the remaining onion half. Sauté the pork in a small skillet over low heat for about 5 minutes until it is lightly golden and renders its fat. Add the onion and sauté it until it becomes translucent. Remove the onion from the heat.

Combine the remaining ingredients to make a sauce. Stir the sauce, salt pork, and onions into the beans. Add 1 cup water to the beans and bake them, uncovered, for 1½ to 2 hours, or until the beans are cooked through, the liquid is almost completely absorbed, and a brown crust has formed. Remove the bay leaf half before serving.

Yield: 4 to 6 servings

MASHED POTATOES

What could be better than mashed potatoes served with meat loaf? This recipe calls for the potato skins to be left on and mashed up with the other ingredients. However, if you prefer, the potatoes can be peeled before cooking for a less homey presentation.

1³/₄ pounds thin-skinned, white waxy potatoes
2 tablespoons butter
¹/₂ cup milk
¹/₄ cup sour cream
4 scallions, the green tops sliced thinly (reserve the white
**   parts for another use)**
Salt and pepper

Place the potatoes in a medium saucepan, and add enough water to just cover them. Bring the potatoes to a boil, covered, over medium heat. Cook them approximately 45 minutes, or until they are soft when pierced with a fork. Drain the potatoes and mash them with a potato masher. Add the butter, milk, and sour cream, mixing them in until thoroughly blended and smooth. Add the scallion greens, salt, and pepper to taste. Serve immediately.

Yield: 4 servings

POTATO PANCAKES

Potato pancakes are a traditional accompaniment for roasted or braised meats. Extra zip is provided by the addition of apple, celery root, and prosciutto to the usual potato-onion mixture.

1 pound white waxy potatoes, peeled
¼ pound celery root, peeled
¼ pound cooking apple, such as Rome Beauty, peeled
¼ pound onion
⅓ cup finely shredded prosciutto ham
2 eggs
⅓ cup matzo meal or cracker crumbs
1½ teaspoons salt
2 tablespoons vegetable oil
2 tablespoons butter

Fit a food processor with the thin shredding disk, and shred the potatoes, celery root, apple, and onion, using medium pressure. (You can also shred the ingredients using a rotary or hand grater.) Squeeze out as much liquid as possible from the potato mixture, a handful at a time, and place it in a mixing bowl.

Add the prosciutto, eggs, matzo meal, and salt to the potato mixture and stir to combine well. The mixture should be fairly stiff and hold together well.

Heat the oil and butter in a sauté pan over medium heat until it is sizzling. Form the potato mixture into 8 pancakes using a ¼-cup measure. Drop the pancakes into the fat and cook them until they are cooked through and golden brown, approximately 5 to 8 minutes per side. Drain the potato pancakes on paper towels, sprinkle them with salt, and serve immediately.

Yield: 4 servings

BASIC BOILED RICE

Here's a recipe that will yield perfect results—if you leave the rice alone while it cooks. The rice can be paired with any number of stronger-tasting preparations in the book, particularly the barbecued and stewed dishes, which have plenty of extra sauce in them.

2¼ cups water
1½ teaspoons salt
2 tablespoons butter
¼ cup minced onion
½ bay leaf
¼ teaspoon dried thyme
¼ teaspoon dried tarragon
1½ cups converted rice

Bring the water to a boil with the salt, butter, onion, and herbs in a medium saucepan. Add the rice and reduce the heat to a bare simmer. Cover and cook the rice, *undisturbed*, for 17 minutes. Remove from the heat and serve.

Yield: 4 to 6 servings

VARIATIONS:
Rice with Almonds, Green Beans, and Mushrooms: Omit the herbs from the rice recipe. Add ¼ cup toasted slivered almonds; 1 cup green beans, cut into 1-inch lengths; and 10 ounces mushrooms, sautéed in 2 tablespoons butter to the cooked rice.
Cajun Rice: Omit the tarragon from the basic recipe. Add ½ cup *each* minced onion, celery, and green pepper, sautéed in 2 tablespoons butter, and 1 cup cooked chicken giblets (gizzards, hearts, and livers) to the cooked rice.

Brown and Wild Rice: Add ½ cup brown rice (Wehani or another aromatic brown rice) and ½ cup wild rice to 2 cups boiling salted water. Allow the rice to cook undisturbed for 45 minutes, or until the wild rice kernels have popped open. Mix in 1 tablespoon butter and 2 minced scallions to serve 4.

·:·

SWEET POTATO BEIGNETS

Beignets are southern fritters. Often in the form of fried dough (like crullers or doughnuts) and served at breakfast in New Orleans, they can be made from any type of ingredient—fish, fruit, or vegetables being some more common ones. These sweet potato and peanut beignets are not as sweet tasting as you might expect. In fact, they are surprisingly savory and would go well with any of the pork dishes presented.

2 medium sweet potatoes
½ cup chopped unsalted dry-roasted peanuts
⅛ teaspoon nutmeg
1 egg
½ teaspoon salt
¼ teaspoon black pepper
1 cup unsweetened shredded coconut
Corn oil for frying

Cover the sweet potatoes with water in a medium saucepan and cook them, partially covered, over medium heat until they are tender, approximately 45 minutes. Allow the potatoes to cool. Peel the sweet potatoes and mash them thoroughly. Remove 1 cup mashed sweet potato. The remainder can be saved for another use.

Combine the mashed sweet potato with the peanuts, nutmeg, egg, salt, and pepper and stir the ingredients until they are well mixed. Place the coconut in a large flat plate or bowl. Using an ⅛-cup measure, form the sweet potatoes into small flat patties (the beignets). Dredge the beignets in the coconut until they are evenly coated.

Heat ½-inch oil in a large frying pan over high heat. When the oil is extremely hot (350°F.), add the beignets a few at a time to prevent overcrowding and fry them until they are golden and cooked through, approximately 1 to 2 minutes per side. Drain the beignets on paper towels and sprinkle them with salt. Serve immediately.

Yield: 12 beignets (4 to 6 servings)

SWEET POTATO-PUMPKIN PUREE

The flavor of sweet potatoes blends wonderfully with pumpkin and pork. This vegetable puree would also go well with any type of fowl or game bird, especially that Thanksgiving turkey or Christmas goose. It is also a pleasant change from the usual "candied" version of this underappreciated and very American vegetable.

2 pounds sweet potatoes
1 cup canned pumpkin
4 tablespoons butter
¼ cup honey
¼ cup orange juice
½ teaspoon freshly grated nutmeg

Place the potatoes in a large pan with enough water to just cover them. Bring the water to a boil and reduce the heat to a simmer. Cook the potatoes, covered, until they are tender all the way through when pierced with a knife or fork.

Drain the potatoes and allow them to rest until they are cool enough to handle. Peel the sweet potatoes and mash them in a large heatproof serving dish. Add the remaining ingredients, adjusting them to suit your taste.

Heat the potatoes in the oven at 350°F. for 20 minutes before serving time.

Yield: 6 servings

GLACE DE VIANDE

Glace de viande, or meat glaze, is a very handy thing to have around the kitchen. Kept in the freezer, it will last for months. And you will always have the ingredients for a quick sauce at your fingertips. To make a *glace de viande*: Double or triple the recipe for Pork Stock (page 18). After you have strained the stock, return it to a wide-mouthed large saucepan. Boil the stock over high heat until it is reduced to a thick, syrupy glaze. (As the stock reduces, swirl it around the pan several times to catch the brown particles that will form along the edge of the pot.) Scrape the glaze into a small plastic container and freeze it, covered.

To use the *glace de viande*: Run a tablespoon under warm water. Dip the warmed spoon into the *glace* and scoop out as much as you need. One tablespoon mixed with one cup water is equivalent to one cup stock or broth.

PAN GRAVY

This is a basic gravy recipe that can be used for any type of meat. Just substitute different stocks as needed—e.g., turkey stock for a roasted turkey or beef stock for a roast beef—or experiment with other sorts of flavorings. If you are using a strong-tasting herb like mint to flavor the sauce, then stick with a more neutral spirit like vermouth or white wine. Fresh thyme would go nicely with a port- or Madeira-based sauce. Make sure to pour any juices from the carving platter into the sauce before serving.

2½ **cups Pork Stock (page 18) or chicken stock**
½ **cup vermouth or 1 cup white wine, port, or Madeira**
3 **tablespoons butter**
4 **tablespoons flour**
1 **tablespoon chopped fresh mint (more or less, to taste) or**
     other herbs
Salt and pepper to taste

Strain and degrease the pan juices from the roasting pan.

Place the roaster on top of the stove, using two burners if necessary. Add the stock and the vermouth or wine to the pan and bring it to a boil. Scrape up any browned bits from the bottom of the roaster as the liquid boils.

Reduce the liquid by a third (to approximately 2 cups). Lower the heat to a simmer.

Melt the butter in a saucepan over medium-high heat. Add the flour all at once to the butter, whisking it continually. Cook the butter-flour roux, whisking constantly, for approximately 3 to 4 minutes, or until it is golden in color. (It is important to cook the flour long enough to avoid a "raw" taste. But if it overcooks, the flour will not bind the sauce properly.)

Add the hot stock and pan juices to the flour in a thin stream, whisking the entire time. Continue to whisk the sauce until it begins to thicken and come to a boil. Reduce the heat. Add the mint or other herbs and salt and pepper to taste.

Yield: 2 cups

PESTO SAUCE

The pesto is needed for the rolled pork loin recipe appearing on page 154 or the Italian meat loaf on page 88. It makes more than enough for use in these recipes and for topping hot pasta.

2 cups (generous) basil leaves, rinsed off and dried
¼ pound Parmesan cheese, grated
1 ounce Romano cheese, grated
2 medium garlic cloves (more or less, to taste)
1 ounce pine nuts
4 ounces good-quality olive oil
2 ounces ricotta or cream cheese
Salt to taste

Add the basil leaves to the container of a food processor or blender and pulse them until they are coarsely chopped. Add the Parmesan and Romano cheeses, garlic, and pine nuts and process the mixture until a paste forms. With the motor running, slowly pour the olive oil in a thin stream into the basil mixture. Blend in the ricotta or cream cheese and add salt to taste.

Yield: Approximately 2 cups

TEXAS MOP SAUCE

Serve this sauce with the Texas-style ribs on page 147 or with any barbecued meat.

2 tablespoons vegetable oil
1 small onion, minced
1½ cups ketchup
2 tablespoons cider vinegar
2 tablespoons honey
2 tablespoons butter
1 tablespoon Worcestershire sauce
1 tablespoon lemon juice
1 teaspoon prepared mustard
⅓ cup water
1 teaspoon kosher salt
¼ teaspoon celery seed
¼ teaspoon black pepper
¼ teaspoon paprika
1 bay leaf
2 garlic cloves, minced

Heat the oil in a small saucepan over medium heat. Add the onion to the oil and sauté it until it becomes golden and translucent, approximately 5 minutes. Add all the remaining ingredients. Bring the sauce to a boil. Lower the heat and simmer the sauce for 5 minutes.

Yield: 2 to 3 cups

VINEGAR BBQ DRESSING

This sauce packs quite a wallop! It is very hot and pungent, but nicely offsets the spiciness of the Carolina-style grilled tenderloin and the but-teriness of the Boston lettuce with which it is served (see page 157). As always, adjust the spices to suit your palate.

½ **cup white vinegar**
¼ **cup sherry wine vinegar**
¼ **cup water**
1 **tablespoon sugar**
1 **teaspoon kosher salt**
1 **teaspoon red pepper flakes**
1 **teaspoon Tabasco sauce**
¼ **teaspoon paprika**

Combine all the ingredients for the sauce in a glass measuring cup or bowl. Taste the sauce for seasonings and adjust it accordingly.

Yield: 1 cup

CONVERSION CHART

LIQUID MEASURES

Fluid Ounces	U.S. Measures	Imperial Measures	Milliliters
	1 tsp.	1 tsp.	5
¼	2 tsp.	1 dessert spoon	7
½	1 T.	1 T.	15
1	2 T.	2 T.	28
2	¼ cup	4 T.	56
4	½ cup or ¼ pint		110
5		¼ pint or 1 gill	140
6	¾ cup		170
8	1 cup or ½ pint		225
9			250 (¼ liter)
10	1¼ cups	½ pint	280
12	1½ cups or ¾ pint		340
15		¾ pint	420
16	2 cups or 1 pint		450
18	2¼ cups		500

SOLID MEASURES

U.S. and Imperial Measures		Metric Measures	
Ounces	Pounds	Grams	Kilos
1		28	
2		56	
3½		100	
4	¼	112	
5		140	
6		168	
8	½	225	
9		250	¼
12	¾	340	
16	1	450	
18		500	½
20	1¼	560	
24	1½	675	

OVEN TEMPERATURE EQUIVALENTS

Fahrenheit	Gas Mark	Celsius	Heat of Oven
225	¼	107	Very Cool
250	½	121	Very Cool
275	1	135	Cool
300	2	148	Cool
325	3	163	Moderate
350	4	177	Moderate
375	5	190	Fairly Hot
400	6	204	Fairly Hot
425	7	218	Hot
450	8	232	Very Hot
475	9	246	Very Hot

24	3 cups or 1½ pints		675
25		1¼ pints	700
27	3½ cups		750
30	3¾ cups	1½ pints	840
32	4 cups or 2 pints or 1 quart		900
35		1¾ pints	980
36	4½ cups		1000 (1 liter)

27		750	¾
28	1¾	780	
32	2	900	
36	2¼	1000	1
40	2½	1100	
48	3	1350	
54		1500	1½

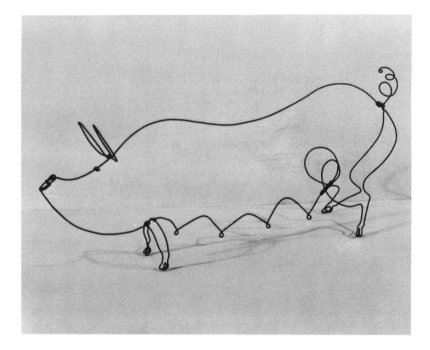

Sow (1928) by Alexander Calder.
Collection, The Museum of Modern Art, New York

BIBLIOGRAPHY

Adams, Ramon F. *Come An' Get It: The Story of the Old Cowboy Cook.* Oklahoma: University of Oklahoma Press.

Arnold, Sam. *Frying Pans West Cookbook: Foods and Drinks from the Frontier.* Boulder, Colorado: Pruett Press, 1969.

Beecher, Catherine Esther. *Miss Beecher's Housekeeper and Healthkeeper.* New York: 1876.

Beeton, Isabella. *The Book of Household Management.* London: 1861.

Boorstin, Daniel J. *The Americans: The Democratic Experience.* New York: Vintage Books, 1974.

———. *The Americans: The Colonial Experience.* New York: Vintage Books, 1958.

Booth, Letha. *The Williamsburg Cookbook.* New York: Holt, Rinehart and Winston, 1975.

Booth, Sally. *Hung, Strung and Potted: A History of Eating in Colonial America.* New York: Clarkson N. Potter, 1971.

Breslin, Ed, and Sean Kelly, eds. *Sty: It's a Hog Eat Hog World.* New York: Vintage Books, 1989.

Burke, Helen. *Food From the Founding Fathers*. Hicksville, New York: Exposition Press, 1979.

Cabeza de Baca-Gilbert, Fabiola. *The Good Life: New Mexican Tradition and Food*. New Mexico: Museum of New Mexico Press, 1982.

Conlin, Joseph Robert. *Bacon, Beans and Galantines*. Reno: University of Nevada Press, 1986.

Cummings, Richard Osborn. *The American and His Food*. New York: Arno Press, 1970.

Drury, John. *Rare and Well Done: Some Historical Notes on Meats and Meatmen*. Chicago: Quadrangle Books, 1966.

Ellman, Richard, and Robert O'Clair, eds. *The Norton Anthology of Poetry*. New York: W. W. Norton & Company Inc., 1973.

Evans, Ivor H. *Brewer's Dictionary of Pharase and Fable,* 14th Edition. New York: Harper & Row, Publishers, 1989.

Farrington, Doris. *Fireside Cooks and Black Kettle Recipes*. Indianapolis: Bobbs Merrill, 1976.

Fussell, Betty. *I Hear America Cooking*. New York: Elisabeth Sifton Books, Viking, 1986.

Gillette, Fanny Lemira Camp. *The White House Cookbook*. New York: David McKay Co., 1976.

Glasse, Hannah. *The Art of Cookery Made Plain and Easy*. London, 1796.

Hilliard, Sam Bowers. *Hogmeat and Hoecake: Food Supply in the Old South, 1840–1860*. Carbondale: Southern Illinois University Press, 1972.

Hooker, Richard J. *Food and Drink in America: A History*. Indianapolis: Bobbs Merrill, 1981.

Janney, Werner L., and Asa Moore Janney, eds. *John Jay Janney's Virginia: An American Farm Lad's Life in the Early 19th Century*. McLean, Virginia: EPM Publications, Inc., 1978.

Jones, Evan. *American Food: The Gastronomic Story*. New York: Random House, 1974.

Kaufman, Alice. *The Centennial Treasury of Recipes of Swiss Mennonites*. Kansas: Mennonite Press, 1973.

Kimball, Marie Goebel. *Thomas Jefferson's Cookbook*. Charlottesville: University Press of Virginia, 1976.

Koehler, Margaret. *Recipes from the Port of Provincetown*. Riverside, Connecticut: Chatham Press, 1973.

Lamb, Charles. *Selected Prose*. Middlesex, England: Penguin Books, 1985.

Lane, Wendy. *The Wall Street Journal*. New York: Dow Jones Publishing, June 20, 1985.

Lincoln, Mary Johnson. *Mrs. Lincoln's Boston Cookbook*. Boston: 1884.

Luard, Elizabeth. *The Old World Kitchen*. New York: Bantam, 1987.

Makanowitzky, Barbara Norman. *Tales of the Table: A History of Western Cuisine.* New York: Prentice Hall, 1972.

McDonald, Forrest, and Grady McWhinery. "The Antebellum Southern Herdsman," *Journal of Southern History.*

Nolan, Aretas, and James Greci. *Pig Raising.* New York: Row Peterson & Co., 1918.

Randolph, Mary. *The Virginia Housewife.* Baltimore: 1831.

Reed, Ethel. *Pioneer Kitchen: A Frontier Cookbook.* Los Angeles: Frontier Heritage Press, 1971.

Roosevelt County Historical and Genealogical Society. *The Pioneer Cookbook: Early Settler Recipes.*

Root, Waverly, and Richard de Rochemont. *Eating in America: A History.* New York: Ecco Press, 1976.

Salwen, Peter. *Upper West Side Story: A History and Guide.* New York: Abbeville Press, 1989.

Sedgewick, John. "Brotherhood of the Pig," *GQ.* New York: Condé Nast, November 1988.

Sillar, F. C., and R. M. Meyler. *The Symbolic Pig.* London: Oliver and Boyd, 1961.

Skaggs, Jimmy. *Prime Cut: Livestock Raising and Meat Packing in the U.S., 1607–1983.* Texas: Texas A&M University Press, 1986.

Solomon, Jack, and Olivia Solomon. *Cracklin Bread and Asfidity: Folk Recipes and Remedies.* Alabama: University of Alabama Press, 1979.

Talmadge, Betty, Jean Robitscher, and Carolyn Carter. *How to Cook a Pig and Other Back-to-the-Farm Recipes.* New York: Simon & Schuster, 1977.

Taylor, Joe Gray. *Eating, Drinking and Visiting in the South.* Baton Rouge: Louisiana State University Press, 1982.

The New English Bible. New York: Oxford University Press, 1972.

Time Magazine, "Night of the Wild Pigs." New York: Time Publishing, June 4, 1990.

Weisberger, B. A. "Beef, Pork and History," *American Heritage.* July/August 1989.

Wilcox, Estelle Woods. *Buckeye Cookery and Practical Housekeeping.* Austin, Texas: Steck Warlick Co., 1970.

INDEX

Ground Pork (*continued*)

terrine of rabbit and, 39–41
see also Sausages
Grunt with a Thousand, 180–81

Ham, 123–37
  baked with Fish House Punch glaze,
    127–28
  baked with maple bourbon glaze, 126
  basic types, 7–8, 123–24
  in black bean soup, 23–24
  Black Forest, and turkey croquettes,
    130–31
  cooking time/serving sizes, 11
  corn cakes with, 175–76
  fresh, with apple cider sauce, 128–29
  pâté, 131–32
  peppery bread dumplings with, 179–80
  prosciutto, in potato pancakes, 183
  prosciutto, shrimp and scallops, 136–37
  slices with raisin sauce, 132–33
  steaks Hawaiian, 135
  steaks with red-eye gravy, 133–34
Ham hock
  in baked beans, 180–81
  in black bean soup, 23–24
  in Hoppin' John, 21–22
Ham Pâté, 131–32
Ham with Fish House Punch Glaze, 126
Ham with Raisin Sauce, 132–33
Ham with Red-Eye Gravy, 133-34
Hash, chicken and sausage, 59–60
Hawaiian Ham Steak, 135
Hawg 'n' Hominy, 20–21
Herbed meat loaf, 87–88
Hominy, ribs and, 20–21
Hoppin' John, 21–22
Hors d'oeuvres
  bacon cheddar crackers, 28–29
  empanadas, 66–67
  ham pâté, 131–32
  pig balls stroganoff, 90–91
  pigs in blankets, 35–36
Hot Dogs, 81–82
  pigs in blankets, 35–36

Indian Pork Burgers, 83
Italian Meat Loaf, 88
  pesto sauce for, 191
Italian Ragu, 52–53
  in zucchini and eggplant gratin, 171
Italian Sausage, 84–85

Jamaican hot pepper sauce, 143, 144–45
"Jerk" Pork Spareribs, 144–45

Jerusalem artichokes, and potato stuffing,
  102–3

Kale, creamed, 168–69
K. C.'s Meat Loaf "Americaine," 87–88

Lamb Sausages with Dried Cherries,
  88–89
Lasagna, chili, 60–61
Legumes
  baked beans (grunt with a thousand),
    180–81
  black bean soup, 23–24
  chili lasagna, 60–61
  Hoppin' John, 21–22
  Portuguese soup, 26–27
  three-bean soup with bacon, 27–28
  see also Green beans
Lettuce
  BLT salad dressing, 30
  North Carolina barbecued tenderloin
    wrapped in, 158
Linguiça, Portuguese soup, 26–27
Loin of pork
  "Celestial" roast, 151–52
  characteristics, 7
  cooking time/serving sizes, 10
  oven-braised, 149
  rolled and stuffed with fennel/red
    pepper, 156–57
  rolled and stuffed with pesto, 154–55
  sliced, sweet-and-sour style, 118–19
  see also Chops; Cutlets; Tenderloin

Main dishes. *See* One-pot meals; Chops;
  Cutlets; Ham; Ribs; Roasts
Maple bourbon glaze, 126
Marinades, 8
  see also Sauces; specific recipes
Mashed Potatoes, 182
Mashed Turnips with Caramelized Shallots,
  172
Meat Loaf "Americaine," 87–88
Medallions. *See* Cutlets
Minted pan gravy, 153–54, 189–90
Moors and Christians, 23–24
Mop Sauce, 147, 148
Mushrooms
  pork ragout with wild, 108–9
  rice, almonds, green beans, and, 184

Negima-yaki, 113
New England Clam Chowder, 24–25
North Carolina Barbecued Tenderloin,
  157–58
  vinegar BBQ dressing for, 193

Potatoes
    mashed, 182
    mashed with turnips, 172
    pancakes, 183
    puree tip, 165−66
    stuffing, Jerusalem artichoke, Swiss
        cheese and, 102−3
    see also Sweet potatoes
Potato Pancakes, 183
Prosciutto
    in potato pancakes, 183
    shrimp and scallops with, 136−37
Prunes
    apple stuffing with, 178−79
    in pork stew, 58−59
Pumpkin and sweet potato puree, 187
Purees
    tips for preparing, 165−66
    vegetable, 169, 187

Quenelles, 38−39
Quiche, Southwestern, 68−69
    chorizo for, 79−80

Rabbit and pork terrine, 39−41
Raisin sauce, 132−33
Ravioli, Chinese, 32−33
Red cabbage, braised, 167
Red-eye gravy, 133−34
Ribs, 141−48
    Caribbean, 143
    characteristics, 7, 8
    cooking time/serving sizes, 10
    and hominy, Southwestern-style, 20−21
    "jerk" (Jamaican), 144−45
    Pennsylvania Dutch stuffed, 145−46
    Texas-style with sop and mop sauces,
        147−48, 192
Rice
    basic boiled, 184
    black bean soup with, 23−24
    cooking tip, 166
    Hoppin' John with, 23−24
    in stuffed cabbage rolls, 33−35
    stuffing with fennel/red peppers,
        156−57
    variations, 184−85
Roast Pork with Sauce Robert, 104−5
Roasts, 141−42, 148−61
    "Celestial" (Chinese-style), 151−52
    characteristics, 7
    cooking time/serving size, 10−11
    crown, with minted pan gravy, 153−54
    rolled/stuffed with fennel and red
        pepper, 156−57
    rolled/stuffed with pesto, 154−55
    sauce Robert with, 104−5
    shoulder/loin oven-braised, 148−49

standing time, 5, 142
suckling pig, 150−51
tenderloin au poivre, 161
tenderloin barbecued North Carolina-
    style, 157−58
tenderloin in sherry-mustard cream
    sauce, 159−60
see also Ham
Roast Suckling Pig, 150−51
    corn bread stuffing, 176−77
Rolled Loin of Pork with Fennel and Red
    Pepper, 156−57

Sage-flavored sausage, 78−79
Salads
    bulgur wheat, 174
    greens with goat cheese and warm
        bacon vinaigrette, 31−32
    see also Dressings, salad
Salsa, tomato cruda, 173
Salt
    curing techniques, 8−9
    in sausages, 75
Salt pork
    in baked beans, 180−81
    in New England clam chowder, 24−25
Sauces
    apple cider, 128−29
    dried cranberry, 106−7
    glace de viande for, 188
    pesto, 191
    raisin, 132−33
    red-eye, 133−34
    Robert, 104−5
    sesame, 32−33
    sherry-mustard cream, 159−60
    spaghetti, 52−53
    Texas mop, 147−48, 192
    tomatillo, 49−50
    tomato-dill, 34−35
    vinegar BBQ dressing, 193
Sausages, 73−93
    bratwurst, 76−77
    breakfast, 78−79
    chorizo, 79−80
    cooking time/serving sizes, 11
    in corn bread stuffing, 176−77
    equipment for making, 74
    hash, chicken and, 59−60
    in Hoppin' John, 21−22
    hot dogs, 81−82
    Italian, 84−85
    Italian with piperade, 86
    lamb with dried cherries, 88−89
    pork and duck, 92−93
    pork and duck pizza, 64−65
    in Portuguese soup, 26−27
    in Southwestern quiche, 68−69

Laurie Platt Winfrey, Inc.